W9-CCM-332

I Run, Therefore I Am—

Nuts!

Bob Schwartz

**Illustrated by
B.K. Taylor**

Human Kinetics

Library of Congress Cataloging-in-Publication Data

Schwartz, Bob, 1960-
   I run, therefore I am—nuts! / Bob Schwartz.
     p. cm.
   ISBN 0-7360-4035-8
   1. Running--Humor. I. Title.

PN6321.R85 S38 2001
818'.602--dc21   2001024831

ISBN-10: 0-7360-4035-8
ISBN-13: 978-0-7360-4035-8

Acquisitions Editor: Martin Barnard; **Production Editor:** Melinda Graham; **Assistant Editor:** Scott Hawkins; **Copyeditor:** Lisa Sheltra; **Proofreader:** Pamela Johnson; **Permission Manager:** Toni Harte; **Graphic Designer:** Fred Starbird; **Cover Designer:** Keith Blomberg; **Illustrator:** B.K. Taylor; **Printer:** Versa

Human Kinetics books are available at special discounts for bulk purchase. Special editions or book excerpts can also be created to specification. For details, contact the Special Sales Manager at Human Kinetics.

Printed in the United States of America

10

Human Kinetics
Web site: www.HumanKinetics.com

United States: Human Kinetics
P.O. Box 5076
Champaign, IL 61825-5076
800-747-4457
e-mail: humank@hkusa.com

Canada: Human Kinetics
475 Devonshire Road Unit 100
Windsor, ON N8Y 2L5
800-465-7301 (in Canada only)
e-mail: orders@hkcanada.com

Europe: Human Kinetics
107 Bradford Road
Stanningley
Leeds LS28 6AT, United Kingdom
+44 (0) 113 255 5665
e-mail: hk@hkeurope.com

Australia: Human Kinetics
57A Price Avenue
Lower Mitcham, South Australia 5062
08 8277 1555
e-mail: liaw@hkaustralia.com

New Zealand: Human Kinetics
Division of Sports Distributors NZ Ltd.
P.O. Box 300 226 Albany
North Shore City
Auckland
0064 9 448 1207
e-mail: info@humankinetics.co.nz

To my wife Robin, my partner forever. To the A team—our children Adam, Andrew and Amy—who have provided me more motivation than they'll ever know. Long may they run. But not faster than me—at least for a few more years.

And to runners everywhere. For we know the secret of life (and it's more than chocolate).

Contents

Acknowledgments

This book has been many miles in the making and I give great appreciation to Martin Barnard, Acquisitions Editor at Human Kinetics, for his keen vision and insight from inception on through completion. Most importantly, he never once attempted to change his e-mail address to avoid my frequent messages. That's tolerance at its highest level.

Many, many thanks to Production Editor Melinda Graham, for her editing acumen, humor, excellent suggestions and her talent in chapter choreography which saved funny lines from the oblivion of the editing room floor. Thanks also to Aisha Ansari, Publicity Manager, for her enthusiasm and efforts and everyone else at HK who had a hand in the process.

Much gratitude goes to B.K. Taylor for his wonderful artwork and superb wit. I also thank him for never throwing his hands up in the air and tossing me out of his studio when my descriptions for drawings appeared to be deliberately vague.

To my older brother, for introducing me to the joy of running and for my mother who was kind enough, on mornings I played Kenyan teenager and ran to school, to carpool with my gym bag and books and meet me there. Thanks to my father for instilling a work ethic and for the annual outings of my youth to the NCAA Indoor Track and Field championships in Detroit where I was first exposed to the finer art of elbowing for position down the final straight (and at the concession stand).

I'm grateful to my wife Robin, who has given me her support and unconditional toleration and love over the many miles. That's no small feat when living with a zealous runner.

Finally, thanks to all the dedicated editors of the magazines who have welcomed my humorous running essays, enabled me to establish an audience and helped make this book possible. Namely: Kathy Freedman/*Washington Running Report*; Jennie McCafferty/*Michigan Runner*; Amby Burfoot/*Runner's World*; Lisa Kireta Schwartz/*New York Runner*; Matthew Nelson/*Tail Winds*; Dan Frederick/*Midwest Running*; Paul Larkins/*Running Fitness*; Matt McGowan/*Run Ohio*; Brook Gardner/*Race Center NW*; Megan Kearney/*FootNotes*; Beth Hagman & Lizzie Wann/*Fitness Runner*; Pete Ireland/*Arkansas Runner*; Jane Hawkins/*Oklahoma Runner*; Joanne Schmidt/*Inside Texas Running*; Lorraine Evans/ *Florida Running & Triathlon*; Mary Lou Day/*Running Journal*; Jen Lyons/*Metro Sports Boston*; Kyle Ryan/*Twin Cities Sports* and *Windy City Sports*; Steve Toon/*Texas Health & Fitness Sports Magazine*; Don Archer/*Missouri Runner*; Kellie Katagi/(formerly at) *Rocky Mountain Sports* and web editors Dennis Brooks/ *www.ontherun.com*; John Elliot/*www.marathonguide.com* and Ken Parker/*www.runnersweb.com*.

And to race directors and race volunteers everywhere, because they can never be thanked enough.

Introduction

Let's proudly admit it. Let's enthusiastically welcome it with open, sweaty arms, ugly toenails, and firm hamstrings. We runners are indeed different! We're the ones who have been known to pour sport drinks on our Corn Flakes and take lengthy showers in our new Gore-Tex running suit to test its water-resistant capabilities. What do you mean, you haven't done that? Well, okay. How about passing out race T-shirts on Halloween from your overabundant collection, along with bite-size energy bars, inspirational athletic quotes, mini-crew socks, and pocket-size pace charts? No?

Hmmm. Well, maybe I am a tad bit more peculiar. All right. How about going agog over the latest edition of your running magazine containing a review of the newest line of training shoes? Aha! You've got to admit that puts your heart rate monitor number into your target zone.

You enjoy basking in the radiant glow of a kaleidoscope of race application forms at the local running store. You delight in refueling on a bruised banana, a half-frozen raisin bagel, and lukewarm electrolyte replacement drink at the postrace refreshment table. In a torrential downpour. At 8:00 on Sunday morning.

These are your stories, to make you laugh about interval training, find the joy in glycogen depletion, and chuckle at your never-ending search to locate your lactate threshold. It's a funny look at all the peculiarities, quirks, and lovely obsessions of those of us whose menu highlight is a new flavor of energy gel, who live for the feel of crusty sweat, and who wear blisters like badges of honor.

I remember, from years ago, the look of a rather portly gentleman who, although perhaps not having run more than six yards in the last 20 years, was kind enough to offer his services as a volunteer at the end of a marathon. You know the ones who are there when you cross the finish line and toss that little blanket of aluminum foil around you for warmth and you feel like a giant piece of shake and bake.

I was pale and doing the lactic acid shuffle while wearing the pained expression of having run the last six miles in the lovely abyss of severe everything depletion. He cautiously approached me with a look of profound disbelief and was undoubtedly questioning the fact that one actually pays a registration fee to participate in this apparent masochism. As I stumbled toward him I couldn't help but joke a little. I looked up at him with a pained expression and harnessed the energy to mutter, "I'm signed up for another marathon next weekend so I was holding back a little bit with this one."

I then lay down on the pavement and he looked at me wondering if I'd lost all semblance of sanity and asked, "You really enjoy this?" Ah, yes. The cardinal mistake of a non-runner. Looking for sound logic from someone who returns from a freezing cold winter run with ice-covered eyelashes, frigid jaws, and a warped, half-cocked arctic smile that mutters through frozen lips, "Rrrrat Rrrras Frrrun."

Rational thought from someone who sleeps with his race number pinned to his shirt for fear he'll forget it in the morning? Someone who gets up at 5:00 A.M. to run 20 miles on a Sunday morning, but can't ever seem to conjure enough energy to get across the family room floor and answer the phone before the eighth ring? Someone preoccupied, before the start of a race, by the crucial issue of whether the right amount of Vaseline was placed on potential chafing areas? You want solid logic from all that?

I then looked at my inquisitive race volunteer and provided him with a kind of deranged look and crazy crooked grin. He took a cautious step back from me at that point. I raised my arm with considerable effort and pointed to the camera taking personal photographs of each runner crossing the finish line. I then summoned enough strength to launch into my best Barbra Streisand impression, singing the theme from *The Way We Were* (with a few modified lyrics):

> "**M**emories light the corners of my mind . . .
> *If we had the chance to run it all again*
> *Tell me would we—'You bet'—could we—'Not right now'. . .*
> *What's too painful to remember from the race*
> *We're so thankful we forget!*"

As I broke into chorus, my fellow runners began looking at me and wondering just what the heck I'd carbo-loaded on. Luckily for all, I stopped short of doing a song and dance number from *Funny Girl*. Didn't quite have the capillary capacity and remaining stamina for that one.

But that was indeed the answer to the inquiry posed by my dubious race volunteer. Of course we enjoy it! We enjoy the memories. The experience. The feelings. From training runs, to races, to running with friends, to going solo in the pouring rain. It's all very rational, at least to us.

If you also can't find humor in tender quadriceps after a marathon, the enervated feeling after a difficult run, delayed-onset muscle soreness, and the challenge of running in a wind chill factor of 40 below—well then, loosen up a little!

The point is, no matter what the circumstances, no matter if we're competitive racers or strictly run-for-funners, we all love it. We keep coming back for our faithful fix. We continue to allow it to occupy our thoughts. We keep thinking, *how, in the name of Joan Benoit Samuelson, can somebody not enjoy this sport?*

To us, it's not really exercise. It's life, and a feeling on which we're hooked. This book is a collection of humorous essays on many topics unique to us, the runners. From the intricate art of drinking from paper cups while on the run, to the equitable concept of virtual training miles, to the *Name That Ailment* game show, to *Kenyan Water Aerobics*, to the unique talents of the Matrix Man of Running Performance, it's a comical examination of a sport that is near and dear to our well-conditioned hearts.

There are funny stories that you'll be able to relate to, whether you're usually in the middle of the pack, up near the front of the pack, or so far from any semblance of a pack you're wondering if everyone went home already.

Whether 23 miles or 3 miles is your definition of a long run, whether you're trying to break five hours for a marathon or five minutes for a mile, it's all the same. Running humor is a universal concept. Hey, what's funny for the gazelle is also funny for the plodder.

For those that love the aromatic smell of perspiration in the morning, who enjoy the exhilaration of exhaustion, who drink solely from squirt bottles, whose wardrobe is over half-filled with clothes having reflective fabric—this book's for you. Yes, we're different. And quite thankful for it.

Humor on the run. What a combination. I think I hear Ms. Streisand singing again. "So it's the laughter. . . ." Yes, it is. The laughter of the long distance runner.

Part **I**

· · · · · · · · · · · · · · · · · ·

Training

Avoiding the Fall From Pace and Belly Smacking Into the Lactic Acid Pool

Chapter 1

· · · · · · · · · · · · · · · · ·

Rules to Run By (Heh, Heh, Heh)

I've had it up to my CoolMax hat. Everywhere I turn there's another marathon training program designed to assist one in easily completing a marathon. Standing. In one piece. Coherent.

Well, it's just not fair to us veteran marathoners whose running history began with not only hitting the legendary wall, but becoming encased in it and staggering to the finish with a demented half-grin.

When we began running marathons, the concepts of lactate threshold training, VO_2max, and heart rate monitors weren't even around. We were the naïve souls of the pre-energy-gel era. The running relics. We proudly wore the battle scars earned from running the last 10 miles of the marathon with mind-altering glycogen depletion producing a lovely hallucinogenic state. That was a true runner's high!

We overtrained, inadequately tapered, and didn't drink or eat properly. Through sheer ignorance we unflinchingly violated every present-day cardinal rule of proper race preparation and marathon running. We went bonk big time, but just assumed that was all part of the process. Delirious was our middle name.

I'm tired of now watching people cross the finish line with a big smile, having done everything correctly from training to pacing to fueling. They don't appropriately display my initial marathon look of having had a tryst with a fast-moving steamroller while pulling an enormous tank stuck in deep quicksand. No, they look tired but not exhausted, thirsty but not dehydrated, slightly sore but not slithering on spaghetti legs. It's just not fair! Where's the delirium? The unfathomable fatigue? This isn't right.

We more seasoned runners need to stick together. We must generously give new marathoners the opportunity to experience the lovely agony we encountered. The complete enervation, the nausea, the cramps, the crater-size blisters. We came, we ran, we withered!

Nietzsche wrote, "That which does not kill me makes me stronger." We'd help them get stronger than ever if they'd only follow our veteran words of advice.

1. Taper, schmaper. Taper? You've got to be kidding. You want to lose that finely tuned conditioning you worked so hard for? That rapid leg turnover? You're a virtual running machine. Cut back? No way. Keep that consistent training going right up until a day before the race. And to gain the psychological edge to go the distance, it's always a great idea to do your last long run a few days before the marathon. This just reinforces that you've got what it takes. Don't worry about "dead legs" come race day, as adrenaline and fan support will overcome that completely.

2. Speedy start. The key to a successful start is to place yourself as near to the front as possible. You want to get caught up in the faster pace of the elite runners and make certain you annihilate your planned pace in those first few miles. This way you'll already be well ahead of your goal target, and the mental boost you'll receive is immeasurable. Just get as far ahead of your target time as quickly as you can, and the stimulus of the race will keep you going the rest of the way. Take advantage of all that pent-up energy in the first half of the race. Go! Go! Go!

3. Bathroom discipline. Let's talk anatomy. You drink fluids; you eventually have to expel. Do you want to have to waste time stopping for a port-a-potty at mile 18? I think not. The key is to forego all fluid offered at the various aid stations. Additionally, you won't lose those valuable seconds by slowing down to grab a drink. Recognize that if you're really thirsty there will be plenty of fluids available at the finish line. That is an extra incentive to get going, as unquenched thirst and a parched throat are great motivators.

4. Caffeine combustion. Give yourself a great big kick-start. If you're a regular coffee drinker, then simply quintuple your normal intake. If you're new to the caffeine connection, then three cups will do you just fine. Don't worry about upsetting your stomach, or the diuretic effects of coffee, as that's quite a small trade-off for a good opening mile time.

5. Try something exciting. You've trained hard and should reward yourself with something new and special for the race. The best thing would be a brand-new pair of shoes, or a different make of socks, or even a new breakfast cereal. Maybe Fiber Flakes or Bran Buds! Mix things up a little for the big day.

6. Uphill, downhill. Attack hills with reckless and utter abandon. Hunch over, lengthen that stride, and sprint up as fast as humanly possible. Get into some solid oxygen debt and then jog leisurely downhill while putting the brake pedals on. This way you'll get the hill out of the way quicker and enjoy the slow pace on the backside while exchanging high fives with the spectators.

7. Goo riddance. Do you think Frank Shorter won a gold medal by downing energy gels or other goos over the last 10 miles? I think not, as the only goo Frank was familiar with in the 1970s was Shoe Goo, and that was something you really wouldn't want to ingest. Don't rely on a shot of strawberry-banana flavored pudding-like food to get you through the sudden lightheaded feeling at mile 20. Just close your eyes and plow ahead. Be a trooper.

8. Postrun recovery. Once you cross that finish line you deserve to simply lie down. Don't expend any further energy; stop the strain train right there. Just take a seat and let those lactic acid pools build right up in your legs where they belong. It may make you sorer tomorrow, but let's just think about today.

If new marathoners would only adhere to these rules to run by, they'd bring a depraved little smile to the face of some old-time marathoners. Heh, heh, heh!

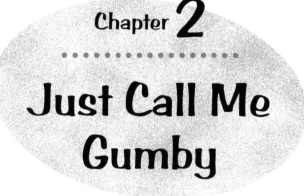

Chapter 2

Just Call Me Gumby

I recall being on vacation a few years ago and giving myself the luxury of having a massage. As my seemingly sadistic masseur was pounding away on the back of my legs, he casually asked, "You're a runner, aren't you?"

I immediately replied in the affirmative, as pride filled my limbs. Like a proud peacock strutting his beautiful feathers, I flexed what I felt to be all my sinewy muscles and concluded he'd noticed my well-conditioned runner's physique. I waited eagerly for the next question, which I assumed would be how many miles I ran that morning.

Guess again, nimblerod! He burst my swelling ego like a pair of too-small Lycra tights exploding at the seams. His next inquiry was "You don't stretch, do you?"

Great, I thought. *Busted on vacation by my masseur.* I immediately blurted out "Yes, I confess—I don't stretch! And I run in worn shoes longer than I should, and I sometimes refuel with no more than a can of diet soda. I've cut a few corners during races, I've lied about my PR (personal record) a couple of times, and I once lined up much closer to the starting line than I should have based on my predicted pace per mile. There—it's all out in the open! Are you happy?"

He gave me a quizzical look as I slowly extricated my stiff body from the table and walked out of my confessional massage. I vowed to change. I'd be back next year and show him the limberness of an overindulgent contortionist. I'd open the door with my feet! I'd lie on his massage table and casually scratch my ear with my big toe! I'd tie my shoes just by bending over at the waist and keeping my knees locked! I'd show him a thing or two about being springy and pliable.

The problem was that I had the flexibility of a steel pipe. The word *stretching* sent shivers down my rigid spine and reverberations through my overly taut hamstrings. Static, ballistic, active, isolated, or dynamic—I'd ignored all types of stretching. I was an equal opportunist at inadequate limbering.

Oh, I'd heard it all before. The benefits of muscles with greater elasticity. Increased stride, less soreness, and muscle relaxation. Easier said than done, when my ability to touch my ankle occurred only when I was sitting in a chair.

> **"I'd be back next year and show him the limberness of an overindulgent contortionist. I'd open the door with my feet!"**

My idea of stretching for an early morning run was to virtually sleepwalk to the end of the driveway and then raise my arms once above my head (and look to confirm I was no longer holding my coffee mug). I'd then bend my neck and quickly glance at my feet to double-check that I had shoes on. Postrun stretching consisted of bending down to pick up the morning paper from the front doorstep.

I'd convinced myself that trying to be limber was painful, and no pain was—well, no pain. But doubts regarding my neglect of stretching began to creep in, as someone seemed to be tying my Achilles tendon a little tighter each night. Additionally, my ability to sit cross-legged was a distant memory, and I couldn't seem to get my socks on without wrestling myself on the floor.

Miraculously, I came upon the answer to my flexibility prayers. I discovered that proper stretching was supposed to stop at the point when it began to feel uncomfortable. Hey, my kind of exercise. No strain, all gain! Perfect. Kind of like an interval workout ending just after the warm-up. This was more up my alley, as I enthusiastically began the journey to limberland.

It was smooth sailing once I figured out the more complicated stretches. This included the one that required placing the exterior edge of your left foot on your right shin and pulling it toward your chest, while contracting your hip flexors, looking over your right shoulder, and whistling "Yankee Doodle" as you exhaled slowly and wiggled both ears in an alternating manner, while pressing your buttocks downward against the floor and rotating your toes in a counter-clockwise direction.

I've gotten more flexible but never have made it back to that vacation spot to show my masseur how I can stand up, grab my ankles with my hands, and then bend over and pull up my socks with my teeth.

I'm thinking of sending him a picture, though. I'll just sign it, *Yours, Gumby.*

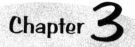

Chapter 3

. . . .

I'm Treadmill Man, Hear the Hum

I've had the luxury of running in the Rocky Mountains as the blue skies welcomed a radiant orange sunrise. I've also felt the misty water from the Oregon coast as I ran along the beach with sea lions sounding in the distance. Leaf-laden paths through the woods of northern Michigan? Been there. Done that. Running on snow-packed cross-country ski trails? A lovely frosty workout.

I shunned indoor running even through frigid winter winds and ice storms. I saw myself as a running purist. An elitist. I needed to breathe the fresh air, experience the natural ground beneath my feet, feel the light snow flurries on my face. But now I must confess and seek natural runner absolution. A few years ago, I defected. I went to the other side. To the land of electronic exercise and artificial light.

I broke my daily rendezvous with Mother Nature and had a regular tryst with my basement. I'd become a treadmill junkie. Slave to the revolving belt, mesmerized by the flashing numbers and beeps, enchanted by the random hill profile program. I traded the sweet smell of spring for the stagnant cellar air, the great outdoors for the great four walls, the warm feel of sunshine for Oprah on my television.

You could have your golden mountain majesties. Just let me run in a climate-controlled environment while viewing ESPN Sportscenter, with my remote control giving me quick musical visits to VH1. Blasphemous? I said sensible. I even had immediate bathroom access. There was no more racing my bladder to the nearest gas station.

My old running buddies would implore me to join them outdoors for a leisurely seven-miler, seeking to entice me with the sweet aroma of clean, fresh air. I'd stick my head beyond the screen door, see the lovely autumn colors, and hear the sound of birds chirping. I wasn't swayed. I was unwavering. I was allegiant. I was an interior aficionado. The beep of my electronic treadmill beckoned me with a loving call. I had to go. The sunlight was beginning to hurt my eyes. My manual speed program was waiting. I warned my running friends not to trip on the uneven sidewalk as I retreated inside.

When I'd been one of the many who actually left their house for a run, I could only estimate the distance I had traveled. With my faithful treadmill keeping tabs, I could conclusively say, "In total, 9.6 miles, with 3 miles at a 6:25 pace on a 1% grade, followed by 2 miles at a 6:00 pace with no grade, concluding with 4 miles at 6:50 on a rolling, level 5 grade, and a cool-down of .60 miles at an 8:00 pace." At that point, my inquisitor would look at me with no real recollection of the question he'd previously asked, while I was about to give my caloric expenditure per hour and my heart rate target training zone information.

I'd experienced the elusive runner's high, churning through a 10-mile trail run with the lovely sights of autumn decorating the landscape. However, once I became addicted to my machine, it was a magical feeling to be finishing 15 miles on the treadmill with George Sheehan quotes decorating the walls, a refreshment stand within reach, and the VCR showing Rocky knocking down Apollo Creed to earn victory. "Yo, Adrian!"

I was the king of the revolving terrain, captain of the shock-absorbent suspension deck, chief of the slip-resistant running surface. Just call me Treadmill Man. Hear the lovely motor's hum.

Previously, when planning a vacation, I made certain there were plenty of scenic running routes available. However, when I was hooked in the land of electronic control panels, I asked questions like, "Does the hotel have a treadmill? With incline abilities? What's the model number? Can you send me a picture of it?" I'd have taken a stay-at-home vacation with treadmill access over Jamaica's beaches without it.

I recognized my race T-shirt collection had diminished, as I'd missed the prior year's 10K races and marathons. However, my PRs improved. If only anyone knew. I couldn't seem to get the local running store to post my times.

I knew my obsession was going a bit too far. I was just one power outage or motor malfunction away from being forced back to the roads. I actually came up with some gradual steps to reintroduce myself to running outside. First, I brought the treadmill and television up to the garage. I turned on a sunlamp and eventually opened the garage door to let in some of that exterior air. Ultimately, I interspersed some quick jaunts around the block with the treadmill workout, trying to coordinate with the commercials.

It was one step at a time to literally find the road to recovery. I found myself beginning to feel nostalgic for open space. I heard James Taylor singing, "I guess my feet know where to take me . . . down a country road." At first I thought, *Maybe,* but then I paused, wondering what the temperature and wind chill were outside.

Eventually, I achieved a balance, with just a bit of indoor treadmill running mixed into the total regime. Hey, Monday mornings in the fall wouldn't be the same without doing a hill workout indoors, all the while watching the National Football League highlights from the day before.

Just me and the purr of my motorized buddy. Hum on!

Republished with the permission of Runner's World/Rodale Press

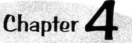

Chapter 4

Around the Learning Curve

Way back when I became a runner, I not only learned about the many potential places one could chafe, but, like cotton sweat pants on a rainy day (not a good idea), I also soaked in all information regarding running.

I began with the basics, learning that *aerobic* is not when your ballpoint pen becomes airborne, and I eventually appreciated *the wall* as something other than an album by Pink Floyd. I discovered that a *tempo run* is not running with a Walkman to the beat of your favorite song, and *glycolysis* was not a new way to remove unwanted facial hair. I also learned that *fartlek* involved periodic fast pick-ups and was not something associated with running soon after having eaten a meal of refried beans.

In becoming a newly inducted member of the neophyte running society, I also gained a fresh appreciation for biology and cytology. Science wasn't my forte in high school; I had struggled like an amoeba out of water. Or was that a protozoan out of soil? Whatever. In a short time, though, I became as comfortable with scientific athletic principles as a well-fitted orthotic in a running shoe.

I read about things such as the importance of a proper cooldown for effectively clearing noradrenaline, an adrenal gland hormone, from one's blood. Heck, before I started running I didn't even know I had an adrenal gland.

I also read that oxygen is the terminal electron acceptor in the energy-generating process of aerobic respiration, which occurs in the mitochondria of exercising muscles. Apparently it's more than just something in the air.

In immersing myself in running-related lingo, I further uncovered that *antioxidants* have nothing to do with the agenda of an anarchist group avoiding oxygen consumption. The term *free radicals* doesn't involve releasing political prisoners, and *pronation* has nothing to with good feelings about your country. Also, *bonk* became known as something other than where British people keep their money.

My molecular biology lessons continued, and I became familiar with the definition of *adenosine triphosphate* as being the immediate source of energy for muscle contraction, as opposed to being the word that knocked me out of the seventh-grade spelling bee.

I also began to learn terminology related to running injuries, and I often engaged in the unilateral game of Differential Diagnosis with my new running friends. They weren't always amused. Apparently a little knowledge can be dangerous or, at a minimum, more than a tad irritating.

I would have previously thought that *chondromalacia* had something to do with time-sharing condominiums in Malaysia. Now, with early-morning studying, I'd not only learned all methods of treatment for this knee injury but I also felt confident that if orthopedic surgery was required, I could do it all by myself in my kitchen.

In addition to appointing myself chief of surgery, I anointed myself commander in chief of the battle against germ infiltration. I became a little maniacal about getting sick and throwing my training off schedule or missing a race. The Centers for Disease Control and Prevention were no longer in Atlanta, Georgia, but in my basement. I learned all about infectious viruses, and I implemented measures to reduce the likelihood of my becoming an unwilling participant in the game of Bouncing Bacteria or Peripatetic Parasite.

I honed the ability to spot someone's runny nose at 100 yards and then steer clear for fear that catching a cold would hinder my long run in a couple of days. I also developed the ability to walk into a room of 50 people and, upon hearing a muffled cough, immediately identify the culprit. Hey, we all have certain skills! Call me the constant defender from contagious conditions! The protector from pathogens! The vindicator from viruses! All right, call my sanity into question.

As time went on, I realized that running terminology was becoming even more scientific with new and improved training methods to help with performance. Granted, there were not yet any technological advances such as a cable car that would allow me to run effortlessly up an 800-yard hill. However, there were workouts designed to increase my ml/kg/min VO_2max while running just below the sudden onset of rapid lactic acid collection, which occurred via the conversion of pyruvate through the anaerobic pathway and, in turn, enabled me to avoid the accumulation of ions interfering with the mechanical contraction process of the muscles, all the while attempting not to exceed the ability of the bicarbonate buffering system via the production of carbonic acid. Something like that. All right, perhaps I could memorize the lingo but was a little fuzzy on its meaning.

I did begin to realize there was a fine line one could cross in accumulating training information. That line of annoyance lies between knowing just enough and going overboard, as you bore to death the uninterested by discussing things like nutritional ergogenic aids to enhance oxygen metabolism, or the optimum recovery ratio of carbohydrate to protein in stimulating insulin levels and glycogen replacement in a synergistic fashion.

I admit that I may not be as exciting at dinner parties with my running-related and scientific training vocabulary, but on the bright side, at least my high school biology and chemistry teachers would be proud of me.

And feel free to send me your questions. For I am Mr. Good Pace, the running science ace.

Chapter 5
. . . .

Kenyan Water Aerobics

I always know when a new form of exercise is becoming fashionable, and it's more than the arrival of a thrilling and captivating infomercial every night at 1:30 A.M. that tips me off.

My theory is based on the Solely Sport Sole principle. Namely, shoes begin to be designed strictly for the newly popular activity. Back when cross-training shoes first made their way to my local sports store, it became clear this was a phenomenon whose time had come. 'Twas the dawn of a running/ biking/ rowing/ aerobic dancing/ cross-country skiing machine/ weightlifting/ stair-climbing/ racquetball/ yoga shoe. Though upon close examination, it looked incredibly like my seventh-grade high-top sneaker. Things have now become slightly more specialized, with specific shoes for everything from indoor rock climbing to stationary bicycling, and the concept of cross-training remains.

When I first became a runner I was a young and enthusiastic purist. I shunned other forms of exercise as inessential. My credo was as clear as my reflective running vest in the dark. If you wanted to be a better runner, run. I was certain Van Gogh hadn't become a better painter by doing papier-mache. He painted. I ran. Okay, his area of expertise was in a slightly different stratosphere, but you get my point.

While I gained more miles under my feet, I continued to be bombarded by the different methods of exercise available. Everywhere I turned there was some new enticing form of physical exertion, or some mechanical contraption designed to strengthen my gluteus to its maximus. But I held tight to my monomaniacal miles-only philosophy. I shunned cross-training, questioning how it could be of benefit if the Africans were such exceptional runners and it wasn't like you ever saw them doing any water aerobics, Tae-Bo, or rollerblading!

Over time, however, I slowly gained the inability to do 25 push-ups without a springboard under my chest. I also noticed a little strength inadequacy when my arms abruptly sank like an anchor from fatigue halfway across the swimming pool, and I had a tough time getting the old quadriceps muscles to kick in and get me out of a squatting position.

It was then that I began to lean toward that heretofore unexplored world of cross-training. The world of complex exercise contraptions sent a little shiver in us machinery-challenged individuals whose knowledge of mechanics didn't go much beyond setting the VCR.

At that juncture, my idea of weight resistance training had been to carry my fully loaded gym bag from the garage to the bedroom. Hey, sometimes it had a heavy, wet towel inside! And at least I could do it one arm at a time. Without a rest break!

While my stimulating internal debate regarding the merits of other forms of exercise continued, something occurred that would cast me right in the middle of the sea of cross-training. My home became the training ground for a miniature Hulk Hogan.

You want to talk about resistance training to improve muscle strength and increase stamina? Ever try to hold down a baby who doesn't want her diaper changed? My continuous wrestle-a-thon with my child (otherwise known as the Diminutive Drop-Kicker) assisted me in resurrecting and challenging certain muscle groups that had gone completely unused since middle school football. Many times I was left sucking for oxygen, lactic acid buildup prevailing in my arms, while my daughter scampered away, leaving me flailing on the floor, waving her clean diaper as the white flag of surrender. Hard interval training had nothing on this workout. She would victoriously thrust her fist in the air and crawl around the room in her birthday suit as she enthusiastically high-fived her mother.

The good news was that over time my upper-body strength increased, but my wrestling skills never really improved. She continued to kick my butt while I tried to clean hers.

As my daughter became older, and potty training pushed out the cross-training of our hand-to-hand combat, I found myself missing the daily strength sessions with my young workout partner. Not immediately finding a father-toddler taekwondo training class for us, I soon found myself at the local health club.

I recall standing quite perplexed in the middle of the exercise room, staring at some industrial-size machinery with enormous control panels, which left me wondering whether a pilot's license was required before operation.

Working out with this type of high-tech equipment was in direct contrast to my running philosophy. I'd always been enamored with the simplicity of the sport that

"Everywhere I turned there was some new enticing form of physical exertion, or some mechanical contraption designed to strengthen my gluteus to its maximus."

was premised on the S-to-the-5th principle. Socks, shoes, shorts, shirt—all set. The minimalist marathoner.

I'd previously concluded that other forms of recreation required too much accoutrement, too much planning ahead, or way too much mechanical understanding. Skiing? Mountains weren't usually found within the subdivision. Tennis? Need someone else on the other side of the net, or incredible speed and agility to play yourself. Tackle football? Shoulder pads, helmets, and 22 people. It's a little hard to round up a good game before work at 5:30 A.M.

But I now stood biceps to atrophying biceps with a complex piece of exercise equipment. I wasn't even exactly sure where I was supposed to sit, let alone whether it was designed to strengthen my trapezius, could simulate a trip down the Autobahn, or was actually the world's largest cappuccino machine.

Eventually I learned about everything from inversion boots to lat pulldowns to dip machines to gyroscopic exercisers. I even confirmed for myself, through an aerobics class, that I have the rhythm of a Mexican jumping bean, as I accidentally turned it into a contact sport for my classmates and myself. Needless to say they weren't overly amused.

I have held tight to some of my running principles, as I've yet to buy a pair of those fancy-dancy new cross-training-type shoes. Although, I must confess, those indoor volleyball/bungee jumping/skateboarding shoes do look pretty snazzy.

I do admit that I felt more than a little pride in developing new muscles. Being a diehard runner, I never thought I'd say anything like, "Do you want to feel my sternocleidomastoid? Or watch me flex my vastus intermedius? And man, are my gastrocnemii like steel cables."

But I did say that. Although I've yet to get someone to want to see me crack a walnut with my biceps brachii. But at least I know I can—even two at once!

Ah, the many and varied talents of a cross-training convert.

Part II

Racing

The Thrill of Victory and the Agony of Da Feet

Chapter 6

· · · · · · · · · · · · · · · · · · ·

Runner Mutation

Mild-mannered, reserved Clark Kent could enter a phone booth and come out as Superman. Any of Mr. Kent's inhibitions were swiftly cast aside, and amazing strength and courage were displayed. (But why Superman could let bullets bounce off his chest and then duck when the empty gun was thrown at him—well, that remains a mystery.)

Many runners also experience a similar metamorphosis when race day arrives. A phone booth is not required—rather, we simply enter the port-a-john and come out as Racing Machine. No flying cape is necessary, nor is a large *S* emblazoned across our chests. However, give us a race number and a few safety pins, tie a computer race chip to our shoelace, point us in the direction of the starting line banner, and suddenly we undergo a personality mutation.

Any timid, demure, or restrained nature is cast aside, and we become unabashed members in the emancipation-from-decorum club. No longer do we feel somewhat unnerved about using a public restroom, as the world becomes our own little fire hydrant. Neither tree nor corner alley nor patch of bushes is safe from an overloaded bladder before or during a race. The world may be an oyster for some, but it serves as a large lavatory for a racing runner.

We can go from our bland, color-coordinated, conservative work attire to wearing every color in the Mercury Paint catalog in our shorts alone. And who's going to carry a handkerchief or tissue along during a race? No way. Suddenly need to blow your nose a little? Just turn to the side, make sure the landing pad is clear, and give a little honk—the runner's shameless method of proboscis projection.

Your prerace routine includes becoming Mr. or Ms. Anti-Friction. You're a walking human lubricant as you fervently lather petroleum jelly on every single potential chafing area. Most significantly, you have no reservation about applying it to any usually concealed body part in front of thousands of perfect strangers. Modesty, shmodesty.

Additionally, no run would be complete without a visit from some of the body's natural cacophony. It's the melody of the runner's short, sometimes rhythmic, and often spontaneous body sounds. We may try to successfully squelch a little burp at the board meeting, but now we feel equally triumphant if a belch reaches the decibel level of a sonic boom and we achieve the trajectory levels of low-flying aircraft with our spit. And clearing our throats? We have no concern if we sound like a cat with a colossal toupee-size hairball.

We also shed all pretenses with our loud gasps, grunts, and pants. Toward the end of the race, we shamelessly

> "Your prerace routine includes becoming Mr. or Ms. Anti-Friction. You're a walking human lubricant as you fervently lather petroleum jelly on every single potential chafing area."

display wheezing which sounds like a lactate overloaded, congested Tin Man from *The Wizard of Oz* trying to start a 1964 lawn mower, with both having had no oil in over 30 years.

We normally exhibit impeccable dining manners, but now we aggressively grab a cup of sport drink on the fly, gulp it down quickly as it dribbles and drools from our mouth, and then forcefully discard a crunched-up paper cup on the sidewalk. Postrace refreshments serve as the catalyst for seeing how many bananas and bagels we can consume in the span of our best 800-meter time. We often burn more calories racing around the refreshment tables than we do during the run itself.

If we cross the finish line with a new PR, we deep-six any semblance of emotional restraint as we repetitively thrust our arms in the air and let out a Neanderthal scream of delight, followed by 47 consecutive resounding shouts of "Yes! Yes!"

Hours later, we've changed out of running clothes, showered, and resumed our more restrained personality. Until the next race. Until they give us another number to pin to our chest. Until we once again emerge as Racing Machine. Look out!

Chapter 7

Not So Scarlet Letters

I always had a bite-the-bullet, grit-your-teeth, and pound-your-chest approach to racing. I also recognized that there were going to be some race days when the powers that be would determine I had no power to be. Those races in which the old biorhythms were slightly out of whack, and that volunteer position of handing out drinks at the initial aid station sure seemed a lot more attractive.

But my credo was that no matter how poor I felt, I was determined I would always finish. Crawling, rolling, slithering—I'd get there one way or another. You wouldn't see me with my T-shirt pulled up to conceal my face as I sat humiliated in the back of a support vehicle driving to the finish area.

The great runner Alberto Salazar was once administered his last rites after he'd plowed ahead and finished a race with heat stroke. Bob Kempainen, 1996 U.S. Olympic Marathon trials winner, literally tossed his cookies during the race, but he never went off stride, let alone off pace. My idols. I, too, was a warrior. I would finish every race, by any means. I was resolute. I was relentless. I was wrong.

Yes, I am here to admit before all that I'm now a card-carrying member of the Did Not Finish Club. Not really a lodge that everyone is clamoring to get into, but at least one that has some talented runners among its constituency, such as Bill Rodgers. Bill and I, combined, have won four Boston Marathon titles (all right, he's got all four) and eight marathon DNFs [did not finish] (but he's got seven of those).

Boston Billy has been smart enough to know when to give in to those little inconveniences, such as the severe dehydration that causes one to feel faint and delirious and see the lovely flashing lights. To paraphrase singer Kenny Rodgers (no relation to Bill):

You got to know when to hold 'em, know when to fold 'em,
Know when to walk off the course and know when to run.
Don't count your race finishes before you get to the end.
You may be only halfway through when your race is done.

Yes indeed, those heretofore dreaded and ignominious three letters, DNF, have now officially followed my name in the race standings. Much to my surprise, I was not immediately ostracized from the local running club and my application for the next race was not rejected and sent back to me with a note saying, *Sorry. We only accept finishers.*

My joining the DNF club all started when I'd read perhaps one too many articles on proper hydration and how it was necessary to take in a sufficient amount of fluids the day before a marathon, especially if the weather was to be very warm.

I was about to run a marathon in the heat of summer and I proceeded to drink water, water, water. My activities the day before the race were then confined to either standing in the bathroom or at the kitchen sink restocking my water bottle. I figured I might not win the race, I might not set a PR, and I might even have to take (for the first time) a mid-race potty break. But I was darn tootin' gonna be the most hydrated runner out there. A regular water buffalo extraordinaire. I'd take accomplishment wherever I could find it.

Well, apparently, a summer of running in the heat without adequate salt replacement had left me a little light on that highly important electrolyte called sodium. Seems my prerace-day lengthy lavatory intervals hadn't really helped the situation. My overindulgent-camel routine had left me a little bit too watered down. I should have also had 1 or 12 salty V8s.

Come race day, the first sign something was amiss was when I didn't need to participate in my prerace port-a-john ritual. This is when, about 46 seconds before the starting gun is to go off, I must bribe the person in front of the bathroom line, as my bladder feels like an overinflated beach ball ready to explode. Seems my condition that day had caused my body to retain all the liters of sport drink I'd ingested that morning, and I felt a little like a waterlogged combination of the Michelin Man and the Pillsbury Doughboy.

The second sign that perhaps this wasn't destined to be a great, memorable experience was when it felt like I'd hit the wall 600 meters into the race. As the first mile unfolded, I tried to settle into a cadence that was in conjunction with the gush, gush, gush sound emanating from my stomach. It wasn't a pretty picture. I had the lovely feeling of a swollen, nauseated whale.

By mile 2, those pesky little DNF thoughts first began echoing in my liquid-laden head. I mulled around the fact that perhaps running another 24.2 miles wasn't the greatest idea to come along that day. But I was a runner—albeit a slower, more uncomfortable version of my former self. I'd been bred on the credo that winners never quit and quitters never win. However, by mile 3, I'd turned to a new page of *Bartlett's Quotations.* I was still coherent enough to recall the quote of Teddy Roosevelt:

> *"The credit goes to the man who is actually in the arena . . .who strives valiantly . . . and who, at the worst, if he fails at least fails while daring greatly, so that his place shall never be with those cold and timid souls who know neither victory nor defeat."*

Yeah! That was it. I was daring and failing and most of all flailing, but at least a step ahead of those "timid souls." Even if I quit. The problem was, before officially becoming a race calamity I needed to get to mile 10, as that was where I was first scheduled to see my family. If I packed it in before then, I'd have left them speculating, when I didn't show up, how I could have become the first runner in modern marathon history to have gotten lost on a straight, well-marked, point-to-point course.

As I plodded forward, it had become quite clear that the only record I'd be setting that day was for being passed by the most runners within the first hour of a marathon. After 139, I stopped counting and simply squished on.

I eventually arrived at mile 10, and there was one slight problem. There, waiting for me, appeared to be the largest congregation of spectators ever assembled in North America. As bad as I felt, I had a little too much stubborn pride to step off the course at that juncture. I feared everyone would go instantaneously silent, collectively point their fingers right at me, and my face would be plastered on that evening's sports news report in the blooper segment.

> **"I also wasn't required to stand on a scaffold in the center of the local running store and receive the hurled insults of customers, nor to wear the scarlet letters DNF on my singlet at all future races of my lifetime."**

In going over the course map with my wife the night before, we had noted that I could easily be seen again either at mile 12 or mile 14. I was now simply praying that she missed me enough to opt for mile 12. She didn't. I trotted on to mile 14, armed with the knowledge that it would be my finish line.

Upon arrival, I stopped running and officially became a Did Not Finish. And you know what? The running gods did not immediately strike me with a bolt of lightning, and I didn't suddenly hear Marlon Brando in *Apocalypse Now* saying, "The horror! The horror!"

I also wasn't required to stand on a scaffold in the center of the local running store and receive the hurled insults of customers, nor to wear the scarlet letters DNF on my singlet at all future races of my lifetime.

I received some medical assistance and was much better later that day after digesting a few gallons of extra-salty salsa. The problem was having to repeat a zillion times to friends just what the heck had happened. After tiring of telling the real story, I opted for advising everyone that I'd actually won the 14-mile race that was held in conjunction with the marathon. No one took me up on my slightly disingenuous offer to see the winner's trophy.

The good news was that it was the best I'd ever felt the day after a marathon. No soreness in the old quadriceps. Amazing what only going about halfway will do to shorten your marathon recovery time.

Now, I don't plan to add to the DNF tally that Bill Rodgers and I share. But the DNF did produce something similar to what I learned after finishing my first marathon. It is survivable. And no one laughs at you. Really.

But you just don't feel quite as justified partaking in the postrace refreshments.

Chapter 8

City of Lard, Here I Come

I may be the only person in North America who based his choice of college and postgraduate studies not on academic reputation, but, instead, on the popularity of running in a particular city.

Yes, I admit that my matriculation was based on a town's level of perspiration. I placed more importance on the total ratio of 10K races to weeks in the year than on the school's student-to-faculty ratio. I gave more significance to running reputation than scholastic standing, and more import to the availability of all-comer track meets over available academic majors. I placed less weight on the courses of study and more on the courses of scenic running.

Thus I completed college in Boulder, Colorado, and then moved on to Eugene, Oregon—two of the running meccas in the United States. Places where you could see a world-class runner just as easily at the local grocery store as on television coverage of the Olympic Games. If Canaan was the land of milk and honey, these towns are the lands of sport drinks and energy bars.

But it wasn't just the elite runners that were cruising around with speed, endurance, and sinewy muscles. The inhabitants of these cities pride themselves on their overall level of fitness, and there was hardly an out-of-shape soul to be found. Before I moved to Boulder, I took some kind of peculiar pride in the fact that while out on my daily run no other runner had ever passed me. (Admittedly, I had to change direction a few times over the years and occasionally resembled a human gyroscope, but my quirky little streak was intact.) By the end of my first week in Boulder I'd developed whiplash from watching gazelle-like athletes whiz by me on a routine basis. The streak was history, and I had to learn to run wearing a neck brace for a week.

I initially blamed it on the altitude adjustment, next on diminished sleep, and then hypochondria kicked in until I was medically cleared for both anemia and mononucleosis. I was forced to succumb to the fact that swift racehorses now surrounded me; I felt like a slow Shetland pony. It seemed as if I'd slid from racing near the front of the pack to the middle of the pack, and that if I didn't keep training, I'd quickly be chasing the caboose.

> "**By** the end of my first week in Boulder I'd developed whiplash from watching gazelle-like athletes whiz by me on a routine basis."

I was actually getting a little faster but just didn't seem to be gaining on anybody. The bar of competition had been raised, and I found myself hanging on by the fraying laces of my running shoes.

Looking at race standings lost some of its allure, as I had to scan farther and farther down from the top to locate my name. I thus worked on convincing myself that running was an individual challenge, rewards were intrinsic, competition was with oneself, and improvement was measured on a personal ruler.

Moving to Eugene didn't exactly improve my finishing place, as I'd simply moved to the sister city for the land of cheetahs. I was resigned to the fact that the closest I'd come to collecting hardware was visiting the local ACO store, not from accumulating trophies from local races. Those would be going to the more fleet of foot.

But once again I told myself that it didn't matter, that my times were improving even if I didn't have a bullet next to my name on the hit parade of race standings. Just enjoy the camaraderie, the fun of the races, the great performances of other runners.

Well, when it came time to leave Eugene I decided that change was in order. Enough of accumulating those little ribbons they give out to the race participants that finish out of the medals loop. My ribbon drawer was filled with every conceivable color, and my collection was officially complete.

The next visit on my running/living itinerary wasn't going to find me racing the Speedy Gonzalezes in Gainesville or Boston. My next move wasn't even going to be calculated on job availability, weather, or cost of living. It was going to be based strictly on the running competition. And the fact was that I didn't want any. This was my theme song:

Home, home on the map,
Where the turtles shuffle and crawl.
Where people don't have speed,
On cake and soda they do feed.
And no one exercises at all.

Don't lead me to where the rabbits dash; just show me where the laggards dawdle. I'd rather be known as the speedy fish in the small, sluggish pond. I needed to locate the unfittest city in America. The town where, per mouth, doughnut consumption was the highest. Where the idea of going to the track meant going to watch NASCAR or greyhound racing. Where they knew less about anaerobic glycolysis and more about the best all-you-can-eat buffets. That was my destination.

Show me the town where, if there were any runners, they were looking to cut the run short, go a little slower, take another day off, refuel with cheese puffs and corn dogs. Where they cared less about artery plaque buildup and had never experienced lactic acid buildup.

It didn't matter to me if my trophy room became well stocked simply because I was the only entrant in my age bracket. Pride, shmide! I'd had enough of the moral victories. Bring me a conscienceless win, but a triumph nonetheless.

I did my research. I found the place where junk-food joints far outnumbered the health clubs and sporting goods stores, where obesity rates were off the charts, where there were no yoga studios or vegetarian restaurants, where bike paths were nonexistent. A town of smokers, overaddicted TV watchers, and full-fat ice cream aficionados. City of Lard, here I come!

"Show me the town where, if there were any runners, they were looking to cut the run short, go a little slower, take another day off, refuel with cheese puffs and corn dogs."

But then I researched a little further and found there were no running stores. There was no local running club, and, most importantly, only one race per year. I could be the fittest among the unfit, but if there weren't many races to win, then what, indeed, was the point? If no one even knew, if no one was going to bask in complete admiration at my colossal achievements, if no one was going to even give two hoots about my trophy room—well, I figured, just forget it.

I'd continue to go where the runners go, where the trail paths are well worn and weekly speed sessions exist. But I decided to put in my calendar that one race date I uncovered in the land of the slothful and inactive. I was determined to travel there and just maybe come back with a trophy to show my running mates.

And even if my friends were more bemused than amused by my achievement, I figured at least I might become the annual kingpin in the City of Lard, and darn proud of it.

But when that annual race day first arrived, I looked around the hotel lobby where I was staying and was flabbergasted to see sleek runners in racing shoes stretching their hamstrings and hydrating their bodies. My God, there were indeed other desperate trophy-seeking souls like me who would stop at no cost, fly across the country, drive over mountains and streams—all to get to a race where they just may break that finish line first.

I figured I could at least take some strange comfort that I wasn't as crazy as I'd thought. I had company. For whatever that was worth.

I'd still trade it for a nice little trophy.

Chapter 9

• • • • • • • • • • • • • • • • • •

Parade Charade

L et's face it: Every distance runner secretly dreams of winning a race. However, for most runners, such wishes are tempered with the reality that they will forever base their performance on the number of refreshments that remain when they ultimately cross the finish line, or the number of cars left in the parking lot.

I, too, was resigned to never hearing the frenzied cheering and rhythmic applause of the crowd as I sprinted toward the out-stretched tape at the finish line. That is, until this past Fourth of July. That's the day my dreams became reality. Well, sort of. Reality is a relative term, and even more so with me as I've been accused of sometimes living in a parallel universe. But, for this event, the old adage *timing is everything* couldn't have been more appropriate.

That July Fourth morning I decided to go for an eight-miler. It was also one of those days that I refer to as my grab-bag training run. You know those times when you're not entirely certain of your body's capacity until you're a mile or so into the run. It's then that you discover if you have the ability to make it a hard tempo run, or if the best you'll have is a slow, easy run. You don't know exactly what you're going to get until you open the package.

Looking for a little diversion on my run, I plotted a course that would take me by a neighboring town's holiday parade. When I arrived, the sides of the streets were lined with spectators. I didn't see any floats or marching bands coming up the street, and I figured they were behind schedule.

I ran along the parade route, and while discovering I had the ability that day for a fast-paced run, I became aware of some light clapping. I quickly assumed impatient spectators were trying to signal that the parade should begin. Before long, the few clapping sounds increased into mild applause and I thought the crowd must have been getting really restless.

Someone then yelled, "Way to go!" —obviously a sarcastic reference to the city's inability to start a parade on time. I couldn't explain so easily why someone then shouted, "Keep it up," as nothing appeared to be falling down. I began to sense that eyes were focused on me, and I tried to nonchalantly check to make sure my running shorts were still in place.

Suddenly, it dawned on me. Someone had erroneously concluded that there was a running race associated with the parade, that I was the leader, and that the parade would begin as soon as the race ended. Once one person started clapping, it became contagious, with the applause spreading down the street like falling dominoes.

Not ever wishing to discourage any admiration (earned or not), and not wishing to disappoint my newly discovered fans, I continued to run down the parade route.

As I savored the moment, I gave my best interpretation of an elite runner. My pace quickened, my shoulders reared back, and my chest thrust out as I displayed an enviable look of sheer grit and determination. I shot a quick glance over my shoulder, pretending to see if another runner was gaining on me. My stride lengthened and my arms swung hard back and forth as I sprinted toward what apparently only I knew was a nonexistent finish line. Such trivial details didn't really concern me.

The crowd believed there was a race, the crowd believed I was winning, and I had a new motto: *Live for the moment*; or, in other words, *Who cares if there isn't a race when you're winning it?* I pressed onward, giving a thumbs-up signal to no one in particular, and pretended to check my watch with a look that said, *Yes, I have just confirmed I am indeed on world-record pace.*

I knew I was approaching the area where the parade was to begin as I saw the floats and cheerleaders lining up. With the crowd's outstanding support, I mustered the ability to kick it into another gear and enthusiastically thrust my fist in the air as my chest lunged toward the imaginary finish-line tape.

The crowd behind me was ecstatic. Several parade organizers stared at me with a look of bewilderment, some with a look of concern for my mental status, and others with an embarrassed look that they had not been informed of a race associated with the parade. I stopped just short of demanding postrace refreshments and a trophy. I figured it was best at this point to jog home without granting interviews.

That day I learned that the race doesn't always go to the swift, but can go to the less fleet of foot (especially when they are the only ones running). I also began looking forward to the next holiday parade. I was thinking that maybe, if I timed it right, I could plant my brother in the crowd to clap a few times as I went by and yell out, "You're looking good!" and then see what happens.

Hey, just a thought. Nothing wrong with creating your own running reality from time to time.

Chapter 10

Introduction to Ingurgitation

I remember many years ago approaching an aid station for the first time during a race. I'd never tried drinking on the run before, as I usually sat for my meals. I hadn't really thought that there would be any difficulty with this undertaking. Guess again, liquid-refreshment face!

I quickly lost the handle on seven consecutive cups and just about ripped the arms off of two volunteers handing out drinks, as I incorrectly gauged my cup grab speed and strength. I soon realized that there's more here than meets the mouth.

I finally held onto a cup and proceeded to take an unintentional and quick shower with a punch-flavored sport drink. As my singlet became stained in red liquid, I seemed to be equal parts sweat and fruit cologne.

I quickly surmised that sometimes things are more difficult than they seem. This was clearly apparent as I gazed into my paper cup and noted the solitary drop of drink that remained. It appeared to be mocking me, indicating, *Buddy, you just spilled the rest of me over your shorts and up your nose and I'm all you got left for the next two miles. Don't blow it.*

After this initial foray into the arena of drinking while moving, I concluded that along with putting distance, speed, stretching, and nutrition into my training regime, I also had to leave ample time for imbibing practice.

To be able to delicately grab a cup of fluid at racing speed and gracefully empty the contents into your mouth is pretty much an athletic event in and of itself. Most of the time the drink goes in every available orifice *but* the mouth. After a race, I often have to explain to my wife why my earlobes have a grape-colored liquid dripping from them.

> "**T**o be able to delicately grab a cup of fluid at racing speed and gracefully empty the contents into your mouth is pretty much an athletic event in and of itself."

Needless to say, it's not the most comforting feeling at mile 20 as you try to fight off glycogen depletion and find that most of your electrolyte-replacement drink just went into your eyes.

It always amazed me how I could move the cup's contents quickly toward my lips and then have it often miss my face completely. The runner alongside me was never the least bit amused about having four ounces of energy drink running off his forehead, courtesy of my inability to hit the moving target otherwise known as my mouth.

I figured that with practice I could get better. My neighbors undoubtedly questioned my family's sanity as I strategically positioned my wife and young children in the driveway, all holding paper cups for me as I ran back and forth and back and forth.

I could only hope that others believed we were engaged in some type of high-tech research experiment. Perhaps testing the body's ability to rapidly assimilate different levels of complex versus simple carbohydrates, and the yo-yo effect of blood sugars. But I'm sure they were thinking *dodo* and not *yo-yo*.

I eventually discovered that the key was to squeeze the top of the cup in half, pour it into the mouth as quickly as possible, hold it there, get my bearings, straighten up the esophagus, and then give it a quick, hard swallow. At first I couldn't hold it long enough to gulp before it found its way up my nostrils. Thankfully, I improved, with due diligence and late-night cup-training sessions with my family in the basement.

I just know that, with my luck, once I truly perfect the art of aid station drink consumption, they're going to go to sippy cups. But I guess you can't stand in the way of imbibing progress.

Chapter 11

Turkey Lemmings

A few years ago, I was a participant in a race that may now be called Follow the Leader—I Think He Knows a Shortcut. The local annual Turkey Trot run had turned into a Turkey Takeoff, as an overcaffeinated, uninformed, and animated spectator gave his best impression of a highly enthusiastic safety patrol person doing a Jim Marshall.

For those who don't recall this great Minnesota Viking football player, in 1964, Jim confidently picked up a fumble and resolutely took off, running 66 yards toward the endzone. Unfortunately, Jim's internal compass was apparently out of sync that afternoon and off he sprinted—the wrong way. His less directionally challenged teammates took off in frantic pursuit, but they couldn't match his speed; he arrived in the inappropriate endzone and scored for the other team. Needless to say, Jim was a little perplexed when the opposing team joined him in his endzone celebratory dance.

Well, Mr. Directionless Spectator, only 40 seconds into the Thanksgiving race, proceeded to take it upon himself to route the runners down the wrong street. Redefining the word *chutzpa*, he'd boldly concluded that the pace car was going the wrong way! His yelling sounded authoritative and his arm pointing seemed quite purposeful. Runners usually exhibit a collective mind in these situations, along with the intelligence quotient of a gnat. If they'd vigorously trained for the race and were shooting for a 10K PR—well, they'd pretty much follow the leaders down into a sewer hole.

Thus, despite many runners' being quite familiar with the actual course, these turkey lemmings all began turning down the wrong street. They figured that if they had a chance to go from mile marker 1 to marker 3 without actually seeing mile 2, well, all the better.

Off the leaders went, and off the witless pack followed. Some of the more perceptive leaders ultimately concluded it was the wrong way (the dead-end street was a good giveaway). They then tried to navigate 4,000 runners over various traffic barricades and through narrow, pothole-laden alleys (kind of an urban cross-country steeplechase event), determined to get the race back on its rightful course. It was the largest, most clueless, fastest-moving, floatless, unintended Thanksgiving parade in modern history.

The back-and-forth, side-to-side movement of the lost and searching pack resembled a kind of enormous inebriated conga dance line. The perplexed lead runners eventually cut through enough parking lots and had sufficient on-the-run caucuses that they ultimately came upon the correct route. Unfortunately, it was a route now lined with an abundant number of race and parade spectators, all of whom had been collectively wondering how an entire race could have disappeared into thin air.

Suddenly emerging from a side street, the unannounced, meandering, and frenetic runners frantically waved their arms and screamed for the crowd to part so that a few thousand of their closest friends could come on through and get back on course. Lounge chairs, baby strollers, and coffee cups went flying as the spectators desperately moved as if raging, out-of-control animals were charging at them. Which they kind of were.

Race officials finally breathed a collective sigh of relief that things were literally back on track after a little east-west-north-west circuitous detour. However, they were quickly dismayed to find that another large group of runners, behind the main pack, had made a second incorrect turn. This mid-pack group had realized early on the transgressions of their Turkey Trot compatriots. They'd reversed themselves and were now heading back toward the other runners in search of the correct route.

Not a pretty sight, as it wasn't the smoothest of moving mergers. It came close to being the first race ever to come to a complete standstill four miles from the finish, while runners vigorously pointed in numerous directions. Majority finally ruled and the horde of wandering runners began to go in a unified and, thankfully, appropriate direction.

The race eventually concluded without any more unplanned and non-scenic side trips. In the end, various participants had run various courses through various streets at various distances. Some ran shorter, some ran longer, and those (like me) who set personal best "10K" times turned a collective deaf ear to anyone who offered that the course might have been slightly shorter than the correct distance. Hey, we'd take a personal victory any way it came. Don't bother us with minor technical details like course length.

Most runners took it all in stride and shrugged off the wayward path they'd explored. But there were some dyspeptic turkeys that acted as though, by briefly becoming a lost Trotter, they'd forever missed their opportunity for an Olympic gold medal and lucrative endorsement contracts. I'm fairly certain these joyless joggers weren't planning to stick around to happily wave at the Mother Goose parade float going by.

And the nameless but clearly turkey of a spectator who started this runaway run with his less-than-accurate finger-pointing? Who knows, but I only hope he's not moved on to air-traffic-controller school.

Chapter 12

Send in the Clowns

In filling up my car's gas tank on my way back from an out-of-town race, I was suddenly shaken from my insightful postrace retrospection (like whether that fartlek workout of 11 weeks ago was too close to race day) by the arrival of a voice. The sudden sound caused me to reflexively pull the handle from my tank. As I stared at the hose, nozzle to face, I unconsciously uttered the words of Robert DeNiro in *Taxi Driver* — "Are you talkin' to me?"

Incredibly, my gas hose was engaging in a monologue as I stood perplexed. I knew the day wasn't getting off to a great start if, by 10:00 A.M., I'd already experienced a less-than-stellar race performance and now found myself conversing with a rubber tube.

It appeared the gas station gurus had concluded that pumpers couldn't adequately entertain themselves for the extensive 2 minutes and 45 seconds involved in filling the tank, and had provided a little audio info to pass this prolonged time period.

My feeling is that if someone wants to join me at the gas pump, either pump, pay, or at least clean out the empty water bottles from my car. Don't play motor fuel ventriloquist seeking to amuse me.

This all reminded me of how the abundance of entertainment at some races has turned into a virtual smorgasbord of performances.

It often begins with the overenthusiastic, non-running, prerace Jazzercise instructor who thinks the idea of a marathon warm-up is five minutes of furiously active high-impact dancing to the theme from *Flashdance:*

> *"**W**hat a feeling, bein's believin'—I can't have it all, now I'm dancing for my life!"*

This leaves me not only wondering for the next 26 miles what "bein's believin'" means, but also thankful that I didn't rip my racing singlet when prerace jitters got me doing a little breakdancing to the infectious melody.

In many races, before you get through the first five miles, you're privy to bands, jugglers, and sword swallowers designed to divert your attention and amuse you.

It seems as if race directors are part entertainment directors as well. The managers of merriment. Maybe it wasn't enough to advertise that the course was pancake-flat, that energy gels were available at miles 15 and 20, and that they'd provide free pictures of you crossing the finish line. Nowadays you could entice potential participants with the Mormon Tabernacle Choir at mile 9, classical piano music at mile 13, the world-renowned Flying Wallendas' trapeze act at mile 16, the famous dancing flamingos and singing parrots at mile 21, and videos of thrilling Olympic Marathon finishes shown on a big screen at mile 25.

Of course, in contrast to gas station pump coordinators, race directors do have a more rational purpose to their assortment of entertainment and attention attractors. Their goal is, partly, to divert the runners from thinking about what they are actually doing, and to disassociate them from any discomfort that might be occurring. Nothing like thinking back on that mud wrestling contest that you just witnessed at mile 23 to make the time seem to go a little faster until you get to mile 24.

I enjoy these diversionary tactics just as much as the next distractible runner, but I recognize that they might be more necessary for other runners than for me. It doesn't take a whole lot to divert my mind. I view my very short attention span as one of the few physical gifts I have for being a runner. I can go on a long run and quickly lose enough power of attention that I'm fairly unaware of the fact I'm actually moving. Hey, it does help time pass a little faster as long as I do, at some point, remember to start heading back home.

On the other hand, this "talent" isn't always quite so beneficial. I've been known to have lost sufficient attention that I think I should be approaching mile marker 13 in a race when it's actually only mile 6. I've also been known to misplace my focus long enough that there have been times I've forgotten I'm actually racing a 5K as I quickly settle into half-marathon pace. It's always a little shocking to see that finish line come up about an hour sooner than anticipated.

It's on those occasions that I wish I had some type of alertness-predictor gauge. I'd know exactly how much time I could allot to a particular task before any form of effectiveness would completely disappear. I could

"**N**othing like thinking back on that mud wrestling contest that you just witnessed at mile 23 to make the time seem to go a little faster until you get to mile 24."

thereby use my diminished focus to its utmost productivity. Knowing my attention level for a specific day would certainly help me in deciding which race to enter. Should I sign up to race the 10K, given the length of my powers of concentration on that particular occasion, or instead, might I be better suited that day for setting a PR in the 200-meter kids' fun run?

I recall reading how American running great Todd Williams used the power of concentration to combat a repetitive side stitch problem. Apparently, the two ligaments that attached to his liver would spasm and provide Todd an uncomfortable side stitch. To combat this, Todd learned to breathe in a two-to-one ratio and let air out only on his left foot impact rather than his right foot. On some occasions I consider myself lucky to remember to breathe, but here was a man who certainly had a solid attention span and a Buckingham Palace guard's power of concentration. The man could focus. He wasn't going to be distracted by the Fleetwood Mac reunion tour playing at mile 18 or the tractor-pulling contest at mile 22.

I do enjoy all measures aimed at entertaining me during the course of a race. They provide a little spice to things. Just stop short of trying to convince me to perform karaoke at mile 19, or play pin the headband on the runner at mile 9. The participatory activity of running the race is sufficient for me.

But don't stop showing the uplifting and inspiring film clips at mile 25, and feel free to send in the acrobatic clowns any time. Nothing wrong with getting me chuckling on the run. I've developed sufficient coordination and power of attention to run and laugh at the same time. Just don't ask me to also open an energy gel packet at that point. I've got my limits.

Part III

The Mindset of the Distance Runner

The Plentiful Peculiarities of the Perspiring Fanatic

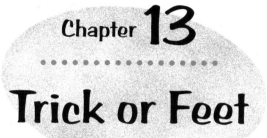

Chapter 13

Trick or Feet

Runners are no different from others when it comes to the two-pronged philosophy of consumption. If something is free, it'll be snatched up irrespective of need. If it's free and edible, it'll be devoured without concern for content or taste.

This latter principle was confirmed when someone placed a half-eaten, trailer-home-size container of cayenne-garlic-flavored popcorn in the kitchen of my office building at 8:00 A.M. Just 24.7 seconds later, not only was the food gone, but someone had also taken a large bite from the bucket as well.

For runners, the *free is wonderful* mentality is best illustrated by an increasingly popular event of race weekends. It's a combination auto show, *Star Trek* convention, and culinary extravaganza for runners. It's the exhilarating, spine-tingling, eye-popping running expo!

There are few things that excite me more than those words. I don't pick races on the basis of flat courses, crowd participation, or course beauty. For me, it's the expo. Better known as racing-brochure paradise, free-energy-gel nirvana, and locker-room-bag heaven. Ah, the bliss of being surrounded by endless choices of moisture-wicking clothing.

I can comfortably reside in the bosom of my running peers, encircled with products and methods to make me run faster, lighter, and pain-free. Where else can I learn about the latest workout to increase my VO_2max to its ultimate genetic capacity, while training at a speed beneath the onset of lactic acid accumulation and improving my capillary density—all the while utilizing the latest heart rate monitor and plugging the results into a new computerized personal training program? Nirvana for the nylon set!

Free merchandise? I've got trinket overload coming from the pockets of my new waterproof, reflective, back-venting, seam-sealed, body-hugging, poly/nylon/microfiber jacket. Can a runner really have too many refrigerator magnets, keychains, bumper stickers, pens, luggage tags, hats, and water bottles with running-related insignias? Never! We are runners, see us accumulate. Forage forward! Halloween has nothing on my large, overstuffed plastic goodie bag full of running treats.

The intelligence of runners is, however, seriously questioned because of their total lack of taste-testing restraint at expos. It's one thing to try a little teriyaki chicken at the grocery store on a Sunday afternoon. It's quite another to have diligently trained for six months for tomorrow's race, and now determine it's the perfect moment to break from the strict training-table regime and ingest items never before introduced to the stomach.

Unable to bypass the joy of free offerings, runners wind up putting harissa-seasoned blue flour corn chips with glycomacropeptides and purified cellulose into their bodies for the first time, all the while washing it down with an inaugural drink of guava nectar. Rational thought is quickly cast aside in the face of free chow.

The multitude of product choices available at expos makes things a little challenging for me, as my middle name is *Indecisive*. I constantly struggle with the epic question of mini-crew or quarter-cut running socks. My footwear selections now explode with choices, including microsafe fiber-optimum moisture management, anti-blister formula, anti-microbial agent, bunion protector, high-density ball-of-foot pads, extra-lightweight ultra-dense thin sole, or breathable elastic-mesh arch. Hey, I have enough difficulty choosing between nonfat, skim, and 1 or 2% milk.

And what would a running expo be without the latest in shoe technology? It took me 10 years and extensive late-night studying before I finally figured out the difference between foot *supination* and *pronation,* and thus the technical aspects of modern shoe science can be slightly complex for me. The expo acquaints me with ethylene vinyl acetate outsoles with air-transfer cushions and graphite roll bars, as well as thermo-polyurethane plates sandwiched in foam with nitrogen bubbles in a viscous substance inserted in the midsole. Yeah, right—just like it looks.

After testing out some foot massagers, toe stretchers, and nighttime foot splints, as well as purchasing a few running shoe ornaments and license plate holders, I make my way past the portable canine water bowl and reflective vest for pets, and exit the expo.

The first leg of my weekend duathlon is complete as I slowly lug my bag of treats to my hotel room. Now, I just have to remember to run that race in the morning.

Chapter 14

A Streak Isn't for the Meek

I used to be a streaker. No, not the kind who felt compelled to share the contours of their bodies, sans shirt and shorts, with a large contingency of unsuspecting onlookers. I mean the other type of streaker (those whose sanity should be even more questioned), who feel compelled to see how many consecutive running days they can place in their shoes.

Of course, this occurs despite days when my own temperature has been hovering around the 103-degree mark, my stomach feels like it's riding 30-foot waves at Waimea, and my equilibrium resembles the wobbling motion of a gyroscope slowing down. Nothing like a quick jaunt around the neighborhood at that juncture to confirm I'm one of the running-afflicted.

What I needed, when I was a running addict run amok, was the assistance of a group of reformed streakers, where I could humbly confess that "I am Bob, and I am a runaholic." I anticipate I'd have been greeted with, "Hi, Bob. How many days in a row you got going?"

In that setting I'd be among my brethren, who had traveled the road of running codependence. Those who ignored minor inconveniences such as broken limbs, pneumonia, and double root canal to get their daily dose of perspiration. Those who shook off nature's blows and braved 12-foot snowdrifts and ice storms to keep their streak of repetitive running days alive. Those who were convinced that darkness would quickly overcome the land if 24 hours passed without their feet moving rapidly in a forward direction. Those who put miles around airport parking lots during layovers, rose before late owls went to bed, and gained a familiarity with the décor of many a gas station restroom, which often served as their locker room on the road.

Eventually I found the middle of the running trail. A compromise on compulsion. I'd like to be able to say I honed into a *the sun will come out tomorrow* philosophy and consciously recognized that I could survive missing a day of running. Nope. Didn't happen that way. I was still many miles away from approaching things in such a logical fashion.

The ceremonial burial of my streak occurred when I adorned myself in running clothing and attempted to briefly lie down on my basement floor as I summoned the energy to get outside. It had been one of those long days when there hadn't been an opportunity to run until well into the evening. My intent was to momentarily rest on the floor and then go for a run to avoid turning into a giant orthotic if the stroke of midnight arrived before I'd put some miles under my shorts.

But I was engulfed by sleep, and my internal alarm clock must have malfunctioned. I awoke on the floor at 1:03 A.M. I immediately broke out in a cold sweat, and hives overtook my body when I realized that on the prior date I'd not sustained an elevated heart rate for an adequate period of time. My God! I'd missed a day of running!

After grabbing a paper bag to fight off my hyperventilation, I rationalized that it was before midnight on the West Coast, and I was therefore within the newly self-created guidelines of technically getting a run in on the prior date. So what if that date only existed 3,000 miles away? The streak was still on a respirator and had the capacity of being revived!

Alas, I concluded that that would be stretching things a tad much. Even for me. I slipped out of my Gore-Tex pants, slid off my running shoes, and removed my Supplex nylon running hat while I bowed my head to observe a moment of silence. The streak had officially bit the dust. Roadkill.

Then something life-altering occurred. I recognized that I was still breathing. And the TV still worked. And the refrigerator still hummed and the wind still blew outside and the stars had not fallen from the sky. Life was actually moving on, despite the fact that I'd missed a run. Comforted with this discovery, I did the only sensible thing. I had a bowl of cereal and went to bed.

During my run the next afternoon, I realized that missing one day hadn't removed all semblance of conditioning from my body. It did not appear, in the technical jargon, that my muscles' oxidative enzyme activity had decreased, nor had my capillary branches gone and taken a hike elsewhere. Miracle of miracles. I hadn't transformed into an out-of-shape blob overnight.

My streak had been prodded by a compulsive daily sweat addiction. I had finally learned that a day of rest from running was survivable.

Now if I could only kick my 12-year streak of having dessert as my dinner appetizer, well then, I'd be all set.

Chapter 15

• • • • • • • • • • • • • • • • • • •

Loony Ways of the Wayward Runner

L et's face it: We runners have a few quirks. Okay, idiosyncra-sies. All right, eccentricities. You want me to admit it? Fine. We can be a little bit nuts at times.

Luckily my wife met me when I was already a runner, but she didn't fully know what type of damaged goods she was receiv-ing. The type that has been known to run a massive number of laps inside the local mall (dodging shoppers) to get a run in on a cold winter day. The type that, to get to work on time the morn-ing after a marathon has to set the alarm an hour earlier than normal. This allows for the additional time it will take to gingerly navigate down the home stairway on overly sore quadriceps.

I admit that I can remember my split time for the 11th to 12th mile of my last marathon a lot quicker than I can remember my mother's birthday. I also admit to placing energy bars in the freezer for enhanced taste and then shattering the early-morning silence by loudly smashing apart the glacial delicacy on the kitchen counter. This sends a shocking shudder through the non-run-ning spouse quietly sitting half asleep at the breakfast table, caus-ing the latter's arms, toast, and coffee cup to abruptly fly to the ceiling. This is my cue to begin my run by sprinting for the safety of the back door. Hey, everybody's got his own warm-up ritual.

I also quite capably demonstrate runner regression by opting for the drinking technique of an infant. I've retreated to the point that I can't comfortably drink out of anything but a squirt bottle. My bottle appears to have been surgically attached to my right hand. Have squeeze bottle, will travel—just make sure to know where restrooms are at all times.

The sanity of runners is also called into question, since we can sometimes be found slowly moving up and down the driveway while staring at a watch. This falls within the ludicrous theory that a run cannot be over until the watch reflects the exact length of time we wanted to run. As I engage in this driveway shuffle ritual, I resemble some type of wayward pinball. I've amazingly convinced myself that the extra 16 seconds I need to reach my "time" for the day does indeed make all the difference in the grand scheme of things. Neighbors do question my sanity as they see me doing my unique up-and-down-the-driveway dance. I find it more plausible to simply tell them it's a new ankle-strengthening exercise that they should try. It's called the Pivot Push Promenade.

Runners are also the type who have been known to meticulously polish and shine their treadmills every three days and religiously wax the revolving belt, but the last oil change and wash for their car occurred some 40,000 miles ago. The skewed priorities of the fanatical.

My car actually resembles a locker room on wheels, with the back seat a virtual closet of running shorts, shirts, and muddy shoes. The floor is piled with a three-inch layer of empty sports-bar wrappers, with a number of old faded race numbers scattered about. There is a year's worth of crumpled running magazines circulating on the front seat, along with a portable mini-bar of electrolyte-replacement drinks. The glove compartment is a runner's haven of miscellaneous needs, as it overflows with half-used Vaseline tubes, reflective vests, safety pins, shoelaces, Band-Aids, and upcoming race applications. (Truth is, a good number of them are applications for races that have already happened without me. My personal record, when finally clearing out the glove compartment, was finding an uncompleted race entry from eight years ago.)

When the car's in motion, there's a constant serenade via the trunk from the side-to-side rotation of an Achilles tendon stretcher, rolling dumbbells, almost-empty bottles of anti-inflammatories, and an old Rolfing stick. Ah, the melodic sound of running-related paraphernalia. It's as soothing as the rhythmic pitter-patter of a runner's feet on a downhill grade.

I've lost all concern for the appearance of my car, otherwise known as my running relief vehicle, since my main focus is directed toward the upholstery not soaking in too much perspiration during the postrun drive home. Maybe Gore-Tex seat covers are an idea whose time has come. And don't give me the choice of spraying my car with new car scent—give me the lovely smell of perspiration in the morning. Smells like victory!

My running-related quirks also allow me to patiently accomplish 18 straight hours of extremely focused perusal and purchasing at the local running store, but I begin to twitch uncontrollably from tedium when accompanying my wife to a department store for over 14 minutes.

Also, place me in a group of fellow runners and I quickly go from Mr. Reticent the Reserved to Mr. Genial the Gregarious.

We runners have our little peculiarities, but that's only in comparison to the others. You know, that unenlightened group called non-runners. We do have the esprit de corps of all being pretty much mini-crew socks residing in the same drawer.

We're all cut from the same long-lasting microfleece cloth, and that's a nice cozy feeling.

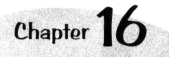

Chapter 16

The Runner's Better Half

Much has been made about the football widow putting up with a spouse who plunks himself in front of the television for games and is enraptured and spellbound for the subsequent three hours. But the significant others of these football fanatics have absolutely nothing on what the spouse of a runner must endure.

A football widow may lose all direct contact with her entranced spouse for a game or two on a Sunday afternoon. Okay, maybe three, if there's a Sunday night game. All right, let's throw in Monday Night Football, the occasional Thursday contest, and even college games on Saturday. She still doesn't come close to matching what a runner's spouse experiences.

I recall my wife's initial exposure to marathon running as she met me at the finish line of a race shortly after we were married. (And no, it wasn't on our honeymoon. Even then, I recognized there are certain limits to which I could push things.) This was one of those races that I hadn't put the required training into, and I shuffled across the finish line more than a little pale, sore, and slightly incoherent. She looked at me in this condition, and not yet fully appreciating the depths of my running insanity, quite cogently stated, "And the point of this is what?"

Over the years she may not have completely grasped the "point," but she's a lot closer, and she's learned to accept my oddities a bit more willingly. The resignation of a runner's spouse.

She now understands that pasta is the staple of all existence and accepts that my life is a perpetual carbo-load. My wife has learned to live with the reality that we needed to build a separate closet solely to stockpile my colossal supply of every type of energy bar made in the free world. She further accepts my odd ability to quote the protein, carbohydrate, and fat content of each one. Truth is, I know more about the RDA percentages of selenium, pantothenic acid, and molybdenum in each of the various bars than I do about the amount of our monthly mortgage payment.

The spouses of runners eventually accept the fact that the kitchen cupboard is filled with 79 plastic water bottles and the silverware drawer has been overtaken by a nearly equal amount of squirt-bottle tops.

Running spouses also learn to live with the laundry room being decorated in drying CoolMax T-shirts and shorts, as more clothes now stay out of the dryer than go in. Running spouses must also acknowledge that we runners are more concerned about rotating our inordinate supply of running shoes than rotating the car tires, we own more waterproof running suits than business suits, and that half our wardrobe has reflective fabric for visibility in the dark.

The spouses of runners also realize that sometimes the timing and destinations of vacations are planned solely around an accompanying race. Any form of sightseeing together is on hold until after the race, and Saturday night's meal won't be at the famous five-star gourmet restaurant in the hotel, but at the all-you-can-eat pasta buffet dinner with free garlic bread at race headquarters.

My wife has agreed to assist me on those less-than-energetic days when it's easier to get a run in if there's a particular destination to run to. She's met me at places like the movie theater, where she's subsequently forced to endure sitting next to my less-than-fragrant body during the show, as I sweat into her popcorn while refueling on a jumbo cherry freeze drink and a big salted pretzel. Ah, the things we do for love.

Spouses of runners also develop the proficient skill of nodding their heads with a feigned look of interest as we go on for the 23rd time about the great training run of that afternoon. They also learn to accept the collect telephone calls that come when we tried running on injuries that hadn't fully healed (having ignored their advice to rest it longer), as we find ourselves stranded five miles from home and pleading for a ride.

They also put up with summer runs leaving us perspiring all over the kitchen floor, as we perform our postrun ritual of sticking our head in the ice drawer of the freezer while guzzling a

> "The spouses of runners eventually accept the fact that the kitchen cupboard is filled with 79 plastic water bottles and the silverware drawer has been overtaken by a nearly equal amount of squirt-bottle tops."

week's supply of sport drink. Runners' spouses also learn to tolerate a 40-minute car detour from our intended destination because we want to officially measure the new course we ran that day.

Runners' spouses eventually accept our devouring a half gallon of toffee crunch ice cream after having done a 20-miler that morning, while we watch our favorite television shows of *Saucony Running and Racing* and *New Balance Elite Racing*.

They also recognize that all forms of communication must temporarily be placed on hold when the weather report comes on the nighttime news so that we can determine exactly what clothes need to be laid out for the morning run. The morning run that invariably awakens them, as we try to quietly tiptoe about but eventually stumble over the minefield of running shoes scattered across the bedroom floor.

Runners' spouses also realize that it's quite common for a runner to be able to run five miles of hard intervals, but then don't ask them to walk more than 200 yards at the mall before they want to sit down. They also recognize that there's no more exciting piece of reading material in the history of periodicals than the magazine containing a description of the new fall running shoes.

Runners' spouses put up with water bottles at the formal dining table, gallon-size Vaseline jars in the bathroom, pins for racing numbers found in virtually every drawer in the house, and a surplus of running socks growing uncontrollably throughout the bedroom dresser.

> "**R**unners' spouses also learn to tolerate a 40-minute car detour from our intended destination because we want to officially measure the new course we ran that day."

They learn to accept the gritty feel and taste of salt achieved by a kiss on the cheek after we return from a run. They also realize there's no need to get alarmed over a slew of black and blue toenails decorating our feet, or our sticking a sterilized pin into the back of our heel to lance a blister. They don't even blink anymore when we implement the postrun, anti-inflammatory measures of attaching bags of frozen peas to our legs or hosing ourselves down in the front yard with a stream of cold water.

They know, from our constant recitation, our best times at every distance from a quarter mile to a marathon, and they accept that we can retrieve those numbers a tad quicker than key birthdays and anniversaries.

Yes indeed, runners' spouses put up with a great deal. But think of the many perks of being married to a runner. Who else can provide 16 incredibly warm quilts made out of T-shirts from races? Who else can report, from the observations of a daily run, anything that's new in the entire community? Who would you want to have sitting in the passenger seat if stranded out of gas on the highway and 10 miles from the nearest exit? Who can hold their breath the longest while searching the bottom of a hotel pool for your ring that slipped off your finger? Who else can greet you with a smile early on a Sunday morning to share a half-eaten blueberry muffin, a lukewarm fruit-punch juice box, and a semibruised apple from the postrace refreshment buffet?

None other than us. Aren't those runners' spouses lucky?

Chapter 17

. . . .

Shoe-Be-Do-Be-Do-I-Did

I t is said that confession is good for the soul. In my case, it's more that confession was good for the soles. I admit, until recently, I'd been a 23-year member of RSO, better known as Running Shoe Obsession. I had more than a slight eccentricity where hanging on to old shoes was concerned.

Some may have a wine collection in their basement. If you'd visited me, you'd have found a shoe cellar. It wasn't stocked with Italian hand-sewn tassel loafers crafted from natural exotic leather, but instead was overloaded with racks of my retired running shoes. We could revisit 1981 together, revel in the full-bodied aroma of the aged synthetic-leather upper and rubber outer sole, and caress the worn heel and tattered laces. Remove it from its box and let it breathe, while reminiscing how that indeed was a very fine year.

I could give you every detail imaginable regarding the personal relationship I had with my running shoes. I could pull out that old 1984 model from the Pre-Advanced Combination Construction era and recite, "The peak of this 13.2-ounce shoe with enhanced motion control and traditional eyelet lacing was setting a half-marathon PR on a point-to-point course. The shoe and I had already experienced some wonderful training runs together by that juncture in our relationship, and I came away from the race completely free of any sign of foot blisters or black toenails. The shoe lasted three more months until replaced by a more attractive, lighter model. But I won't ever forget what that shoe and I had together in the summer of '84."

Truth is, I'm not an obsessive collector of all things, and don't need an off-home storage facility to maintain my running-related magazines and race T-shirts. Nonetheless, with running shoes, I had the mentality of the pack (rat, that is) and couldn't part with any shoe in which I'd comfortably traveled more than 10 miles. By that point, a personal bond had been created. We were attached at much more than just the foot. The end of some relationships often warranted a tearful ceremony before delicately placing the shoes in their tomb of a shoebox. But then something changed.

I read a story on more beneficial uses for old running shoes than stockpiling them and boring friends with a tour of the shoe cellar. I knew that each time I moved on to the latest in running shoes, like some pathetic footwear philanderer, that there might be some more miles left in my prior pair. Nonetheless, I stored them away, and had an inability to completely say shoe sayonara.

But then my compulsion came up against my compassion. I saw an article with pictures of young runners training without shoes, and learned that there were organizations that would collect, size, clean, and ship used shoes to these hardworking athletes. I realized there comes a time when even the strongest of obsessions must come to an end.

As I packed the last pair away, I shed a small tear upon a recently occupied toebox. I knew that they'd be going on to a better life. They'd breathe the fresh air again, feel the trails under their carbon rubber soles, bask in the warmth of a loving touch on their heel counter. It was time for me to cut the proverbial shoelace.

But before I went to the Post Office, I decided to do what any longstanding member of RSO would do. I grabbed the video camera.

Give me a call sometime if you want to see the cinematic chronicle of my life with running shoes. It only lasts 14 hours.

There are many people, both locally and around the world, who would be able to put your old running shoes to good use. Please contact your local homeless shelter, for instance, or your running club may have a recycling program. Some other addresses of programs that help needy individuals around the world and accept donations of used running shoes (in reasonable condition) are as follows:

Shoes for Africa
Mike Sandrock
c/o Daily Camera
P.O. Box 2223
Boulder, CO 80306

World Shoe Relief
c/o Dan Hamer
P.O. Box 423
Trabuco Canyon, CA 92678

Kenya Shoe Expedition
4910 Braes Valley Drive
Houston, Texas 77096

Chapter 18

How Many Virtual Miles Do You Have?

*"**J**ust remember this: No one ever won the olive wreath with an impressive training diary."*

Marty Liquoiri, former American 5000-meter record holder

That's good to know. I was never one who kept a diligent training diary. A penetrating analysis of my training would generate the following cerebral information: If I have energy, I run hard; if I am tired, I run slowly; after a good night's sleep, I throw in speed sessions; and if I can get up early enough, I go long. All right, maybe it's a little more planned than that, but I don't necessarily sprint to my desk drawer to record everything postrun.

The most factual information I ever wrote down concerning my running was the appropriate size of shoelaces to purchase when they broke. And that only happened after too many times of buying laces that left enough slack to tie the bow around my waist. A scientific examination of my running would reveal the simple maxims, *Don't do speed work if your fever is above 101 degrees* and *Don't try to run long the morning after dinner at an all-you-can-eat salad bar*. Nothing too profound.

I always seemed to have just enough energy to get to a race on time, and I usually had sufficient reserves to walk back to my car after the run without too much assistance from other racers.

But this was all before I had children. Once kids arrived, things started to change in more ways than one. Seems I was exerting a lot more energy apart from running and, with our second child (who had a nighttime ritual of sleeping no more than 96 consecutive minutes in a stretch), I joined the ranks of the perpetually pooped parents. Hard as I tried, my schedule didn't allow me to join my son for his morning and afternoon nap.

As the years went on, and the number of slow days between the fast running days seemed to increase exponentially, I decided to do the unthinkable. I started to keep a training log in an effort to uncover some information that might be of assistance in regaining lost energy. After a few weeks of keeping a diary, and noting how my weekly miles weren't as overwhelmingly impressive as I may have imagined, I realized that I needed to include virtual miles as well. It was only fair.

Admittedly, these miles weren't real, on-the-road, true miles but they were, in my opinion, worthy of recording. They were things that either generated some cardiovascular effort or were real miles that were run with a reality handicap.

On any given week, my training diary looked something like this:

Sunday: Planned to go for a long run of 20 miles. Did a short run of 2 miles. Baby teething. Up every hour through the night. Think I slept through the last mile of run. It was the somnolent shuffle. Not sure how I made it home. At least I think this is my home. Need sleep.

Two miles in this condition equivalent to 10 miles after full night's rest.

Total: 2 miles (10 virtual miles).

Monday: Shut off the alarm at 5:00 A.M. Internal debate until 5:03 A.M. Back to sleep at 5:04 A.M. Tried to go on my lunch hour. Ate lunch instead. Tried to go once I got back home. Played two games of Monopoly Junior, helped with math homework, played six games of one-on-one basketball. Put running shoes on. Went to sleep on floor.

Total: 0 miles (1.25 virtual miles from basketball games).

Tuesday: Seven hours of solid sleep on family room floor. Beautiful! Woke up in running clothes with shoes on. Out the door immediately. Ran hard. Two miles warm-up, six miles fartlek, one mile easy. Felt great! Flying over the road! Rejuvenated! Refreshed! Life's wonderful! Played at pool with kids for two hours.

Total: 9 miles (1.5 virtual miles from equivalent water activities).

Wednesday: Stayed up too late the night before. Not enough sleep. Feel awful. Devitalized. Exhausted. Reviewed yesterday's entry. Wish that enthusiastic guy would just shut up. Had to run in morning since kids had soccer game in evening. Dragged myself through seven miles. Felt old. Dilapidated.

Total: 7 miles (1.75 virtual miles from one hour moving around the soccer field, as referee didn't show and I volunteered—dumb move).

Thursday: Sore from refereeing soccer game. Aimed for P.M. track intervals during Little League baseball game. Did eight repeat 800-meter runs at 5K pace; 2-minute rest between sets 1 and 2; 10-minute rest between sets 2 and 3 (watched Adam at bat—he fouled off a lot of pitches); 2-minute rest between sets 3 and 4; 15-minute rest between sets 4 and 5 (ground ball hit Adam in nose, needed to go assist); 2-minute rest for the remaining 3 sets. Three-mile cool-down back home. Indigestion on the way and nauseated at the end. Might be related to eating the extra post-Little-League-game snacks of two jelly doughnuts and a fruit punch.

Total: 7 miles (3 virtual miles, having run the cool-down with extreme difficulty given the lead doughnut belly and sugar high).

Friday: Andrew came along on bike for a tempo run of 8 miles. Shooting for 49 minutes. At 2 miles had pit stop for him. At 3-mile mark, chain came off bike and needed to be fixed. At 4 1/2 miles he needed a drink. At 5 1/2 miles went by his best friend's house and required quick hello. At 7 miles he accidentally clipped his bike mirror against fence. Needed to stop and reattach. At 7 1/2 miles he had to rest his rear end from sitting on bike too long. At 8 miles arrived back home.

Total: 8 miles (1 hour, 47 minutes—58 minutes off goal, but legitimate excuse of accompaniment by seven-year-old; 1.5 virtual miles for being on my feet the additional time).

Saturday: Easy 4 miles in morning. Resting for long run on Sunday. On legs all day to do the following: watch two soccer games, one baseball game, one T-ball game; clean garage; grocery shop; walk with baby stroller; Rollerblade for 1 hour with kids; 45 minutes of catch; one touch football game; four roofball games; one game of capture the flag; half-hour bike ride.

Total: 4 miles (11 virtual miles—not much of a rest day, although personal best for daily virtual mile total).

Sunday: Gave it a shot. Made it to the park (1.5 miles). Found park bench. Lay down. Visualized long run. Went to sleep. Ran 1.5 miles home. Beautiful morning.

Total: I don't care. A lovely virtual run.

Reviewing my running logs didn't lead to any new training strategies. However, uncovering the concept of virtual miles allowed me to see the inequities of awards systems at races. Oh, sure, they have age division awards, but how in the world can I compete with those who have the opportunity to follow a planned training schedule? Or those who didn't run around all afternoon, in 90-degree heat, working the sack race at the elementary school field day, the day before the big 20K race?

I eventually gave up my real mile/virtual mile training log when I was unsuccessful in convincing race directors to calculate and give awards for virtual race time.

At least virtual miles provide me the luxury of convincing myself that if virtual training were not part of my regime, I'd have the opportunity for more rest, and I could be putting in 120 actual miles weekly to be a world-class runner.

Ah, the art of virtual rationalization.

Chapter 19

Mind of the Lost

Runners are known for being a little fixated in their approach to things. Truth is, perhaps a bit fanatical. Maybe even considered a tad monomaniacal. You know those runners who have run the exact same course every day for an eternity at exactly the same time of day, and those who tie and untie their shoelaces 47 times until they feel just right.

Well, a couple of years ago it dawned on me how extreme I'd become. There was no point in attempting to hide what was then painfully obvious.

It seemed that somewhere between running my first marathon and my oldest child turning seven, I'd become culturally illiterate. Reverse evolution. The older I became, the less relevant information I retained. If time is a thief of memory, I'd been royally fleeced. I didn't immediately determine that this had anything to do with running. But it did.

My road to awareness (or my lack thereof) all began when my son asked me a few questions about Pocahontas. I knew she was a Native American, but that just set me on equal footing with my son. After my lack of an adequate response, he next shifted his inquiries to a Mr. Smith.

I then felt a little surge of confidence, as I knew a lot of famous Mr. Smiths. Heck, there was Tommie Smith, the 200-meter gold medalist at the 1968 Olympics; and Geoff Smith, who won back-to-back Boston Marathon titles in 1984 and 1985; or John Smith, the famous sprint coach; as well as Tracy Smith, the former indoor world-record holder for three miles. I was rolling. A virtual repository of critical facts.

My son informed me that he was inquiring about a John Smith who was associated with Pocahontas. I guess he wasn't referring to Maurice Greene's track coach. My momentary feeling of certitude was abruptly erased. Suddenly, I realized that my problem was not that I had brain depletion but, rather, too much time spent reading about glycogen depletion. I was well versed in the subject of running, but it was that big vast world beyond lactic acid buildup that I'd apparently lost a little contact with over the years.

My spare reading material had concerned itself more with knowing famous Mozambique female 800-meter runners rather than refreshing my knowledge of famous Civil War generals. I knew a lot more about VO_2max and the past winners of the New York City Marathon than I knew about trigonometry or winners of the Nobel Peace Prize.

My mind was a virtual warehouse of insignificant running-related trivia. Accumulating this wealth of running knowledge had apparently pushed out the more redeeming data. Runner's repletion had produced a slow and steady erosion of scholarly soil, which yielded a diminution in my educational crops.

The old info escaping from my memory bank wasn't that Alvin Kraenzlein won four Olympic gold medals in 1900. Oh, I'd retained that bit of erudite information and instead lost the knowledge about the Monroe Doctrine or William Jennings Bryan.

I could provide the entire resume for Lynn Jennings' cross country running career, but, in the category of American politicians, apparently Mr. Jennings Bryan was a forgettable fact. I knew a lot more about sprinter Bullet Bob Hayes than President Rutherford B. Hayes.

I figured Pocahontas must have been pushed out of my memory space when I was also filing away the important knowledge that Gerry Lindgren won the NCAA cross country championship for Washington State in 1967, 1969, and 1970. Why couldn't my son have wanted to know about him?

I needed to re-educate or risk being exposed by my seven-year-old. It was like the old story *The Emperor Has No Clothes*. This was more *The Runner Has Limited Recall*.

Slowly, I began to recognize that balance was the key to it all. Running requires the balance of hard days, easy days, speed work, and long distance. I needed to balance in a little educational tune-up with my exuberant penchant for running-related topics.

Given my general lack of free time, I decided I needed to be efficient. I'd always shunned running with a Walkman, but now I concluded that I could do a refresher course on the run with audiocassettes. Maybe an hour of studying while running every day would keep me half a grade ahead of my kids. Okay, probably by the time they reached middle school I'd have to move that to an hour and a half to try to stay up on the more difficult subjects. On the bright side, my weekly mileage would be increasing nicely. Maybe I could set some PRs as well as raise my IQ.

It all sounded good, but I soon discovered that it wasn't very tantalizing or uplifting to be doing a hard interval workout while trying to digest a history of the War of 1812.

A long run sure seemed a lot longer when it was done to a discussion of the construction of the Panama Canal. Somewhere around mile 10 I was pretty much down to listening to every fourth sentence. By the end of the run, I couldn't even remember hearing whether they'd ever actually finished building the darn thing!

I next began to try to scan the encyclopedia (children's version) when I had a free moment, but I kept getting that gravitational pull toward the Olympic games section.

I did learn some new things. Like in the 1904 marathon, the trainers of Thomas Hicks of the United States provided him, over the last 10 miles, a lovely drink of brandy, strychnine, and raw eggs. Apparently they'd not heard of any more conventional method of electrolyte replacement. Despite this concoction, Mr. Hicks still finished in first place, but arrived at the finish line staggering, dazed, and extremely delirious. It took him four days to recover and, upon regaining his senses, he retired from running. I only hope that someday my children will want this critical piece of information to share at show and tell.

Despite a little resurrection of my scholarly data, some things don't change. When the questions from my kids are a little more significant than "What year did Abebe Bikila win his first gold medal in the marathon?" I still do what I used to do. I tell them, "Why don't you go ask your mother that one? And can you hand me that new history book of famous Central American and Jamaican track and field athletes of the 1970s and 1980s on your way out?"

Hey, I'll be ready to impress somebody if I'm ever asked about Byron Dyce or Ana Filedia Quirot. You just wait.

Part IV

....

The Runner's Multiple Skills

Abilities Uncovered in the Unbearable Heaviness of Breathing

Chapter 20

Tegla Take Two

Tegla Laroupe. That's Kenyan for "not of this world," or "we can't be made from the same protoplasm." This was my reaction upon first hearing that Tegla, who (at present) has run the fastest marathon time for a woman and was planning to attempt a double at the 2000 Olympics. And the double she was talking about wasn't running the marathon and then three days later dragging her weary post-marathon body off to watch a scintillating basketball game between the United States and Angola.

She was actually going to race the marathon on a Sunday and then show up on Wednesday for the women's 10,000-meter heats. Showing up for me at that juncture would consist of lying on the infield of the track, half-heartedly stretching the old hamstrings and munching on Three Musketeers bars. For Tegla, it seems she equated showing up with actually racing.

Three days post-marathon, my list of attempted goals usually includes draining toe blisters, finding parking spots close to my destination, and cutting down to three naps per afternoon. On my register of fun, racing a 10K at that point ranks somewhere between an afternoon of watching reruns of *David Cassidy: Undercover* and mowing the lawn with broken scissors.

Apparently Tegla doesn't adhere to the principle that one should rest one week for every mile raced. Oh, you say that's one day—well, whatever works for you. My immediate post-marathon accomplishments include rolling out of bed and having my quadriceps hurt a little bit less than the day before as I engage in a 15-minute backward shuffle down the stairs toward the anti-inflammatories and my vibrating massage chair. The closest I get to anything resembling a "double" at that juncture is a double espresso.

Now I know that many years ago Emil Zatopeck actually went Tegla one better. He won the Olympic 5,000 and 10,000, and then, since there was nothing to watch a couple of mornings later other than equestrian dressage and preliminary rounds of badminton doubles, he thought he'd kill some time by jumping into the men's marathon.

Not content to drive the official race vehicle, he actually won the darn thing, and later called it the "easiest race of my career." That statement clearly explains the difference between the immortals and me. I've yet to meet a race that would fall anywhere in the vicinity of "easy." And winning anything of consequence takes me nearly back to my first-grade field day 50-yard dash contest, where all my competitors went in the wrong direction.

I do have one thing in common with Emil. It is said that his power of determination led one observer to say that his pained facial expressions while running looked as though he was "one who was just stabbed in the heart." This is a fairly good description of my general appearance for the first two weeks after a marathon. And that's just while I'm sleeping.

Back to Tegla. I think I've got her figured out. This was simply a masterful psych job on the other Olympic marathoners. Perhaps she was saying, "I'm going to be in such great shape come marathon day that I'll be able to go for another gold medal a couple of days later. And not on the Kenyan handball team, sister. I'm talking 25 speedy laps around the track. Lace 'em up."

I could only think, *Well, you go, girl!* If I'm her competition, after first questioning her sanity, I'm spending time wondering about her superhuman stamina. I can't seem to generate the same concern when I show up at a local race and say to the one other competitor in my age bracket, "Hey, fella. I'm in such good condition I'm considering cleaning the garage after this race. Both sides." That's my Sunday double.

In first learning about her Olympic quest, I thought if it came to pass on September 27 that she wasn't lined up for the first heat of the women's 10,000 meters because she was still recovering from her 26.2-mile race of three days before, then I'd be able to relate to her just a little more.

If I eventually found out she was recovering by channel surfing back in her Olympic dorm room while scarfing hoagies, washing them down with orange soda, and contemplating what ice cream to have for dessert, then I'd know we're really not that much different after all.

But apparently we are. Tegla did indeed finish her Olympic double. Unfortunately, she was bothered by food poisoning in the marathon, but she battled through sickness and still finished under 2:30:00. I get a similar type of severe indigestion just thinking about the fact that she showed up for the 10,000-meter trials days later. Unbelievably, in the finals she went on to run a time just a few seconds slower than her personal best.

Now it wouldn't surprise me if the 4' 11", 82-pound powerhouse doubled again in the 2004 Olympics. Heck, with her unique approach to post-marathon recovery and her superhuman athletic ability, Tegla could probably qualify for kayaking and taekwondo as well.

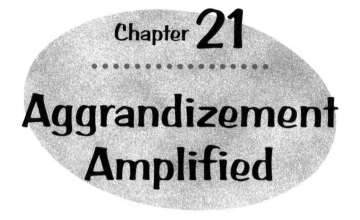

Chapter 21

Aggrandizement Amplified

*"**I** don't exaggerate. I just remember big."*

Chi Chi Rodriguez, professional golfer

One talent that some runners display, even more than being able to flex a rock-solid quadriceps muscle, is puffing. I don't mean the rapid panting from an out-of-control, frenetic sprint to the finish at a 10K race where you probably should have entered the 5K. Rather, it's the puffing done to exaggerate one's running-related achievements (or perhaps the lack thereof).

We all know a runner or two that has their fanny pack overstuffed with enough braggadocio that there's barely room for energy gels. Humility is as absent as a finishing kick in a marathon that you started way too fast.

These runners are also quite skilled in the application of fabrication. Some runners just can't help themselves in adding on numerous nonexistent miles when someone asks how far they ran that day, or inflating by, say, a few decades the number of consecutive running days they have going.

When it comes to talking about their running accomplishments, it takes no more inducement than saying "hello" for them to describe every quarter mile of their last marathon experience. It's a wee bit dubious how that race was run in gale-force winds, with a torrential downpour and hail, on an uphill course—and despite just getting over the Hong Kong bird flu and having an unmerciful sideache from mile 6 onward, they persevered in the face of seemingly insurmountable adversity and set a personal record by five minutes. Yeah, and my name is actually Kip Keino.

Over the years, I've received some interesting holiday cards from these prevaricating people. You know the ones that also include a letter, which fervently details all of the past year's amazing accomplishments by some old running partner and his family who moved away (and of whom I have only a faint recollection).

The letters from these overecstatic, boasting runners often resemble the following:

Dear family, fellow runners, and those others who are somehow lucky enough to receive this holiday greeting letter,

This past year was a fantastic, spectacular, phenomenal year for our clan. Life is so wonderful, so prosperous, so stupendous and astounding that everything feels like an effortless downhill run with the wind behind our backs. What good would it all be if we didn't have the opportunity to brag to you about it? If you can't share in our family's success and accomplishments, as well as perhaps be a tad bit jealous, then what is the point of all the great things going on in our life, really?

Anyway, the family just got back from scaling Mount Everest, after spending a few weeks putting in the miles through Kathmandu and implementing a running program with the local children. We had to pull our boys (8 and 10 years old already) out of their matriculation at Harvard and Yale for a few weeks, but they were able to keep their track and field scholarships going. Their professors let them go with the agreement that the kids would co-teach a graduate-level molecular biochemical kinesiology class next term, which will also research vertical oscillation in long-distance runners and eccentric contraction of the foot arch via landing force. They'll take a couple more weeks off next spring to complete their goal of running across the United States and, in turn, raising 6 million dollars for charity. We'll provide an update of their amazing feats of endurance in next year's letter, or you can track their progress by visiting their Web site at www.we-are-great.com.

My lovely wife had an unbelievable year. She's been in our brand new, 5,000-square-foot basement laboratory, putting her extensive grant to use by expanding on her doctoral dissertation work and exploring the fast-twitch versus slow-twitch muscle fibers of Ethiopian distance runners. She's also doing some work with the International Olympic Committee on new scientific breakthroughs in the area of drug testing, but I can't discuss that further. It's very hush-hush.

Her success continues with her running, as she was able to finish 47 marathons this past year with each one establishing a new personal best time. All that, despite running 95 miles per week and never having tapered for any race.

"Some runners just can't help themselves in adding on numerous nonexistent miles when someone asks how far they ran that day, or inflating by, say, a few decades the number of consecutive running days they have going."

Where does she get the energy? She's also working on the creation of a new fabric that will, to say the least, completely revolutionize the running-related clothing industry. Ever want to run through a frigid snowstorm with a thin, light, one-layer outfit? Just wait.

The exciting news of the year was that our new baby girl set a few world records for 10-month-olds by becoming fluent in Swahili as well as being the youngest person to ride a unicycle while juggling three tennis balls. Most importantly, she also displayed the family talent for running activities by establishing an age-group world record for the 200-meter dash. It's so cute seeing her zip around the track in a spandex onesie outfit. Talk about your overachievers!

Please note our new return address, as we've moved again. The kids were playing around in our upstairs laboratory and came up with a new synthetic material for the midsoles of shoes, which will never lose its high level of cushioning or shock absorption. A major manufacturing company purchased the patent and, needless to say, it was time for us to purchase a new house in the exclusive gated running community I'm sure you've read about. Talk about your scenic running trails! Just outside our back door we've got wood-chip paths that go on for miles and miles. Nothing like seeing the sun rise through those tall evergreens, while deer gallop along in the distance and eagles fly overhead. The community has even hired people to hand out drinks and call out split times at every mile on training runs. I can determine my pace down to the 10th of a second.

"If you want to know more about our running escapades of last year, email us at we-love-us@the_best.com. How any family of runners could be having more fun than we are is beyond our comprehension."

If we invited you over, you'd get a chance to see our new indoor 400-meter track, which rests below our Olympic-size swimming pool and next to our fully equipped 2,000-square-foot exercise room. It certainly is easier to stay motivated when every amenity of the most elaborate health club is found within one's home. And I can't say enough about our full-time trainer, who resides and works exclusively with our family.

Well, enough about everyone else, as I need to tell you about me. After once again improving my marathon time and setting PRs in every race from 3Ks on up, I felt my continued success just wasn't providing enough of a challenge, so I'm doing 50-mile races. Quite amazingly, I haven't lost one yet. I must have some type of unique ability for those endurance events. Go figure.

I'm sure next year will be just as great as this one, and here's hoping that you too can experience even just a little of our happiness. If you want to know more about our running escapades of last year, email us at we-love-us@the_best.com. How any family of runners could be having more fun than we are is beyond our comprehension.

Try to enjoy the new year, and good luck with your running. I'm sure you'd be overly elated if you could experience the joy of improving just half as much as we have. If you'd like one of our autographed T-shirts with a family photo of all of us crossing the finish line at the Western States 100-mile race, well, just give a holler.

It's so wonderful to be on the inside lane and have the feeling of lapping everybody in the track race of life.

Take care now, and happy hamstrings to you.

Chapter 22

· · · · · · · · · · · · · · · · · · ·

Get Your Groove Thing

If running is going to continue to grow in popularity, we must move with the same mutual purpose and collective effort as the giant centipede at the Bay-to-Breakers Race. We must spread the joy of sweat. We must become the evangelicals of endorphin enjoyment. We must sermonize about the wonders of stamina and galvanize others with the actual joy that can be found in glycogen depletion.

But we must first address a problem within our own ranks. We've successfully combated imposters like Rosie Ruiz, who determined that crossing the finish line of a marathon is just a tad easier when you jump into the race at mile 24. Modern ingenuity has given us everything from computer-chip technology to energy bars with flavors other than burnt cardboard. We've even eliminated the 40-pound, rain-soaked, cotton sweat pants with the arrival of waterproof running suits.

But there's a bigger problem than the 12-minute milers sneaking to the front of the starting line to rub elbows with the elite and causing a 62-body pileup when the gun goes off. I'm talking about the thing that does more to deter the neighborhood *my-middle-name-is-easy-chair* non-exerciser from joining the ranks of the running converted. It's appearance that's keeping some folks away. It's not the fear of putting anchor-size thighs in spandex running tights, nor is it the panic that racing singlets are a required accessory. Instead, it's the appearance of anguish they see from a few of us.

We can preach until we go into oxygen debt about the ability of running to feel like the lightness of motion without effort. The fact remains that some non-runners have been erroneously educated. They have viewed those among us whose running style would be best titled *The Unbearable Heaviness of Breathing*. Those whose grimaces resemble one who's been sucking on a lemon for six weeks straight while running barefoot on hot cinders with red ants in their shorts. Suffice it to say that these runners aren't exactly exhibiting a look of genuine joy.

Their grunting and groaning simulates a cross between a wounded donkey and a hyperventilating hyena, all the while sounding like they're 12 yards away from full respiratory arrest.

Their running style is to accentuate every step with a less-than-delicate, earth-shattering foot plop and stare at the ground as though receiving continuous encouragement to keep their feet moving in a forward direction.

It's not that they enjoy their running any less than others do, or are necessarily in poorer condition than, shall we say, the more agile and fluid runners. It's just that they haven't necessarily found the groove. The rhythm of the run. The jig of the jog.

We must help them, for, unintentionally, they're singing to others a bad rap. Their minds may be thinking, *this is fun, fun, fun,* but their bodies appears to be saying, *I wish I were done, done, done.* They look as though they're actually plowing through the pain of stress fractures in every joint below the navel.

We must loosen them up. Unhunch their shoulders. Uncork their squinting eyes and furrowed brows. Stifle their bellowing gasps and lighten their foot plant. For we are all united members of the Pied Pipers of Running Recruitment.

But wait a minute. Perhaps we should just leave them alone. Maybe they are the best procurers of new runners. That's it. It's reverse running psychology they're employing. Their running style may be attracting others with its awkward rhythm as it says, *We welcome one and all.* Maybe they have indeed found their comfortable cadence, and they dance to the beat of a different runner. Hmmm.

I guess we need not try to change the appearance of the gaspers among us. What's good for the gazelle may not be good for the plodder. Perhaps the runner's recruiting motto is more appropriately voiced as this:

"Give me your heavy footed, your less than nimble. Your couch potatoes yearning to be in shape. The woefully inactive in their reclining chairs. Send these, the apprehensive and uncertain among us. We'll guide you joyfully into your comfortable running groove!"

That's it. One person's grinding gait is another's graceful dance. To each his own. To thine own sole be true.

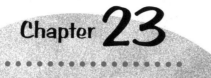

Chapter 23
You Can't Lose Me Now

We runners have heard the ludicrous comments before. From those who wouldn't know the difference between a hamstring and a ham sandwich and think the iliotibial band plays swing music from the 1940s. Those who are much more familiar with Planter's peanuts than plantar fasciitis and believe endorphins are a new type of fish-egg delicacy.

You know those skeptics with the silly inquiry, *How can running be enjoyable if I've rarely seen someone running with a beaming smile?* (I usually tell them that's because the facial muscles are the first to tire in long-distance running and, rest assured, those runners are indeed enthusiastically grinning on the inside.) Or perhaps they question just what the purpose of running is if you're going to wind up in the same spot you started.

But those of us who find some warped comfort in delayed-onset muscle soreness, and proudly display calluses like medals of valor, simply shrug off these comments knowing the nonbelievers just don't understand. Never will.

Better health, weight loss, more energy, and increased stamina apparently aren't enough to convince them of the sensible nature of running. Well, if they need an even more practical reason, I've got it.

It all stems from the prevailing thought that with modern means of travel, communication, the Internet, and cellular phones, the world is becoming a much smaller place. It's just as easy to find out who finished in fourth place in the 1600 meters at the local high school girl's track meet as it is to uncover next Tuesday's dinner special at a mid-priced vegetarian restaurant in downtown Copenhagen, Denmark.

However, my recent revelation was that if the big picture was getting smaller, then for some, the small picture was getting bigger.

It all began when I went to visit an old running friend. We often had traveled to out-of-town races together, and accurate directions had never been his forte. He felt he was a natural homing pigeon when, in fact, he was more like a perpetually wandering puppy. When he provided me directions to his new house in a city a few hours away, I held out the faint hope he'd at least keep me in the same time zone.

After driving in circles for a while, I wasn't so sure. Once lost, I stopped and questioned people working in their front yards. In mentioning specific street names, I'd get a befuddled look, as if I were inquiring about the name of a pastry shop in Istanbul. I declined one gentleman's sign-of-the-times offer to go plug it into the computer to see what came up.

I proceeded to drive around a little bit and finally stumbled on the street I was searching for. Much to my amazement, it was but three short blocks away from those I'd just questioned! My theory was born.

The world may seem smaller, but for some, their immediate surroundings are becoming very large. Namely, their own neighborhood.

These people were clearly not runners, as they didn't seem to venture beyond their borders long enough to know what streets were within a football field of their home. Runners, although winding up where they started, at least know where they went.

Having run various courses from my home over the years, I can tell you even more than just street names within a 10-mile radius. I can provide the color of the front door knocker of that Tudor house, which is on the street with the three homes having detached garages, a marginally uneven sidewalk on the west side, and the German shepherd dog who is outside between 4:00 and 6:00 P.M., all of which is exactly 5.46 miles away.

This practical neighborhood knowledge gained through running also includes the ability to provide the exact location and water temperature of every available working water fountain in the county, and knowing which gas stations require you to factor in the few extra seconds necessary to obtain a key to use the bathroom.

I can also provide a topographical map of the area including any hill higher than a curb, and I know exactly how many seconds I have to get to approaching intersections in order to be able to cross the street as the light changes to green. From the experience of long runs at dawn, I know which convenience stores are open 24 hours and also have my favorite flavor of sport drink, as well as which direction the wind normally blows on an autumn morning.

Is this practical enough for the nonbelievers? Maybe. But we runners can take comfort that we know what lies in the vast frontier extending 200 yards past the family room.

But, most importantly, if you don't know where you're going, you'll never know when you get there. We, with the internal atlas and strong capillaries, are clearly in the know.

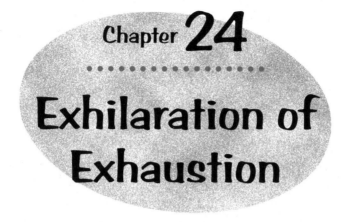

Chapter 24

Exhilaration of Exhaustion

Here are a few simple facts. If you run hard enough, you will get tired. If you run long enough, you will get tired. If you run hard and long enough, you will get very tired. Lastly, if you try to run hard and try to run long and you're not in shape, you are very silly.

Runners know what can occur when we push ourselves to the extreme and perhaps beyond. It's that feeling. Not the gliding-along-effortlessly-as-if-landing-on-feathers-and-propelled-by-a-neverending-source-of-power feeling. Instead, it's the laboring-along-painfully-as-if-landing-on-hot-rocks-and-no-propulsion-left-in-your-energy-pack feeling. And you know what the really funny part is? We elect to keep booking return visits to this lovely location. We're frequent fliers extraordinaire.

I realize that one is indeed a runner even if he limits himself strictly to the easy, comfortable runs a few days a week. Those who solely enjoy this type of running may see those of us who gasp for air at the end of a difficult race or workout and think, *We feel your pain.* But what you're really thinking is, *It'll be just fine if we sit over here and watch your agony from the comfort of the bleachers.* You may feel our pain but cordially decline to have any part of it.

On the other side of the torture track, there are those of us who at some point in our running career initially experienced a certain level of—shall we call it—discomfort. This feeling was registered within our brain and became part of our running remembrance forever. Despite being armed (or legged) with that knowledge, what compels us to keep doing interval workouts when, at times, our arms feel like we're wearing a cement-filled straitjacket and our legs feel like they're encased in lead pipes with a backward gravitational pull?

What drives us to keep trying to train and race at full tilt, knowing the potential exists for a rendezvous with—well, how else can I aptly describe it—displeasure? Nah. That doesn't do service to what we actually plow through. A few aches? No, that's not quite descriptive enough. Distress? Getting closer. How about PAIN? True. At times. How about TORMENT? Now and then. How about MISERY? Well, that may be a wee bit over the top. We do have our limits. At least, I think most of us do.

It's really more that we're a wonderful running contradiction of terms. We actually enjoy sufferable suffering. We willingly tolerate acceptable anguish. We love tolerable tribulation. Allowable annoyance. How about an okay ordeal? How about permissible pain? How about wonderful woe? How about taking a mental health day and getting this problem checked out? Not necessary. We're quite aware of this paradox; no need to see a pair of docs.

G. Gordon Liddy, of Watergate notoriety, actually summed it all up quite well. He was extolling his mental toughness while holding his hand in a candle flame and said, "The trick is not to mind it."

Now I do believe that the vast majority of runners have sufficient common sense to avoid incandescence. The habit of holding your hand in a flame seems a tad bit excessive in attempting to build a little internal fortitude. We runners recognize the challenges of running on a daily basis, and we know that, when we put ourselves in a position of working through some discomfort, there is a certain sense of satisfaction, of accomplishment, of *I did it!* We do learn "not to mind." And it's a wee bit more satisfying than seeing how long your hand can impersonate a candlewick.

Former Stanford University and Olympic track coach Brooks Johnson said, "Pain is your friend." Well, if that be the case, at the end of a tough run we're immersed in a plethora of new play-mates. We know what can, might, does, and will happen to us when we dip full tilt into the elbow grease with all our append-ages. Especially when we're a quart low on available glycogen. Especially when we turn a deaf ear to that little voice in our head that says, *Yo, Road Runner. Enough already. How about we pull back on the throttle, ease it into a slow cruise control, and head straight home for a nice hot shower, a bowl of warm oatmeal, and a chocolate milkshake.*

We do find a certain sense of peculiar enjoyment in the exhila-ration of exhaustion. Go figure. It was once said, "Personality is born out of pain." If that's accurate, then we runners are quite the per-sonable bunch of characters.

In exchange for our dauntless efforts, we get to bask in the glow of a wondrous race or workout. Is there no greater feeling than the sheer joy of stumbling though the race chute at the end of a marathon? Of lying down on the infield grass of a track after feeling nauseated for the past five miles of hard speed work? Of doing another hill repeat when our lungs feel like G. Gordon Liddy's hand doing his pyrotechnic impression?

Well, perhaps I exaggerate a little. But let's face facts. If we wish to improve our speed, enhance our endurance, and bring down those race times—it doesn't happen by going for a leisurely 15-minute walk three times a week, taking long bubble baths, and

> "It was once said, 'Personality is born out of pain.' If that's accurate, then we runners are quite the personable bunch of characters."

sleeping in late on Sundays. It takes effort. It takes persistence. It takes dedication. It takes a willingness to feel a little hurt. It takes (without necessarily feeling the palm of your hand burn) an ability not to mind. And if we don't mind, then it don't matter.

We learn to embrace discomfort. Endure it. We learn to enjoy a little inconvenience on the road of rapture. We have faith that the gods of running will lead us not into the temptation of stopping, and deliver us from the evil of unexpected side stitches and muscle spasms.

And running is abundantly more fun than testing your mettle by using your fingers as a candelabrum. G. Gordon Liddy should simply try running a marathon. It's a heck of a lot more gratifying, and access to the postrace refreshment treats doesn't require using your hand as a fondue stick.

Part V

Nutrition and Recovery

The Search for the Holy Snail and the Joy of C3—Couch, Chips, Clicker

Chapter 25

On My Way Back to Candyland

Becoming a runner usually leads one through the search for the Holy Snail, or whatever nutritional product of the month is purported to bring you greater speed, endurance, or even the improved ability to remember your split times.

Chinese women runners were known to seek assistance by devouring a particular type of worm, which I've yet to find available from aid stations at local races. Japanese runner Naoko Takahashi claimed that a drink based on the stomach acids of giant killer hornets was "a crucial factor" in helping her win the women's 2000 Olympic Marathon. I just haven't gotten the stomach to trap some giant hornets and do a little surgery on their intestinal tracts.

Water used to be the only thing provided during a race, but runners now have choices of various sport drinks, fast fuel gels, fruit, bagels, candy, and cookies. Aid stations are beginning to resemble upscale mini-marts or restaurants. I'm waiting to hear someone yell out at the mile 19 aid station, "Hey, runner 1298, your raspberry-kiwi-yogurt smoothie order is ready. You want chips with that?"

I'd read about Bill Rodgers' affinity for 4:00 A.M. mayonnaise raids on his refrigerator, as well as a winner of the famous South

African Comrades ultra-marathon consuming marshmallow crème as his prerace meal. In the search for greater endurance, I figured I'd give something similar a whirl. I went for Miracle Whip and Rice Krispie treats sandwiches, but, ultimately, they didn't seem to generate more stamina—only sticky fingers and gastric reflux.

I continued to experiment, and also began prodding my children to jump aboard the wheat-germ-and-sprouts bandwagon as I spooned bee pollen over their Cheerios. I viewed one of my parental duties as a kind of Svengali nutritionist, and appointed myself chief deputy of diet. I figured I'd mold their eating habits, and we'd soon be scarfing down chunks of wheat gluten and sucking on ginger cubes. Guess again, Mr. Macrobiotic Man! Welcome to the real world of a kid's penchant for strawberry-flavored milk and glow-in-the-dark macaroni and cheese.

While I'd been drinking down the kefir and dusting spirulina powder on my artichoke salad, I had attempted to bring my children along for the ride on the race track of nourishment. But as I attempted to shake the fabric of their bon-bon world, they preferred living in a Willie Wonka biosphere. They marched to the sound of their own candy wrappers, as they preferred cruising down Rocky Road into Loompaland.

I realized that with food, my children had their own internal calling, and the words they were hearing weren't *broccoli* and *tofu*. While I viewed my running body as a temple, they viewed theirs as party central. I looked for the health store with whole-wheat pasta, carrot juice, and quinoa grain; they were after the local Dairy Queen, Nestle's Quick, and frosted Pop-Tarts. The great divide of the nutritional gap stood between us.

Oh, sure, my wife and I were pretty much in charge of what our children ate in our house, but it was that junk food world on the other side of the training table that garnered our concern. The world of Little League snacks of double-fudge brownies and ice cream at 9:30 A.M. on Saturday morning.

When my children began to show a desire to accompany me to weekend races, I was more than ecstatic. I figured the running bug was biting them, and in addition to improving their cardiovascular system, they'd soon be joining me for a prerace bowl of wheat flakes and crispy whole flaxseed. Wrong again, cauliflower brain!

My excitement was dashed by the realization that it wasn't the allure of the race, the camaraderie of the running community, or even the free T-shirts that kept them coming back. No, it was the abundant supply of doughnuts, cookies, and 1% fruit drinks being offered after the run. I was their round-trip ticket to a free, all-you-can-eat buffet of sugar-filled morning snacks. They were using me big time. I never even had to drive them home from the race, as their elevated body sugar gave them such a potent buzz and hyperactive hallucinogenic state that they preferred running alongside the car on the way back.

After having tried unsuccessfully to sneak brewer's yeast onto their Chee-tos and Brussels sprouts onto their fluorescent-like Velveeta, I was forced to concede that my children ranked food strictly by the pleasure principle. Saturated fats and cholesterol levels weren't so high on their list of immediate concerns. The more nutritionally bankrupt something was, the more they enjoyed it. This operated under the law of sugar and demand.

Something finally dawned on me as I continued to see my children hit the ground at a full sprint in the morning and go non-stop until they'd hit the pillow at night. I realized this was all on a diet fueled less by polenta and more by Popsicles. I began to wonder whether my devotion to celery juice and pomegranates was actually translating into better race times and more energy.

In trying to capture a little more of the stamina and speed of my children, I looked at their dietary history and concluded the following (sung to the tune of "This Old Man") was abundantly clear:

This little boy
He's turned one.
He tasted ice cream on his thumb.
He's now asking for a triple scoop cone,
And wishing Candyland were his home.

This little boy,
He's turned two.
He loves going to the zoo.
It's not the elephants that bring him glee.
It's the zoo's slurpees and cotton candy.

This small child,
He's turned three.
He wants sweet things constantly.
He zooms around like a Tasmanian devil clone.
Beware, this child's entered the sugar zone.

This big boy,
He's turned four.
He loves cookies, begs for more.
"What's for dessert?" is his constant refrain,
Three innocent words I've come to disdain.

This growing boy,
He's turned five.
Pleads he needs sugar to stay alive.
I thought rice and veggies would do just fine.
He claims doughnuts are his lifeline.

This little man,
He's turned six.
For breakfast he needs his sucrose fix.
Cereal with green marshmallows is quite the sight,
He claims it's vitamin-fortified so it's all right.

This old dad,
Just back from a slow run.
He wants half the energy of his son.
Is it all the sweets that make him go?
Could be—so pass me some of that cookie dough.

This running man,
Almost 40 and a Master,
Still searching for ways that he can get faster.
I realized food moderation might be the key.
I'm now having chocolate eclairs with my green tea.

Now don't get me wrong. I still value good nutrition and continue to wash my glucosamine complex sulfate tablets down with beet juice, drink my ginseng, and search for a magic potion. But, now and then, I do substitute Cocoa Puffs for my carotenes and Tater Tots for my turnip greens.

Most importantly, I can still eat more Twinkies at one sitting than my children can. That's even more impressive to them than my best marathon time.

Chapter 26

It's All in the Drool

As I watched the head of my friend (who was training hard for a marathon and had run his first 20-miler that morning) teeter back and forth at the dinner table, I unconsciously began mimicking the motion. It was just a few moments until his eyes slowly shut. What followed was his abrupt awakening when his head plopped into his warm mashed potatoes. As he looked up and shook the gravy from his eyebrows, his food-encased face said, *What just happened?*

My only thought at that moment, as I assisted in spooning him off, was, *Now perhaps you'll listen to me, O pigheaded one.* I thought that given the lovely swan dive into his dinner plate, he'd finally be willing to heed my admonitions regarding the conservative pace he should run on his long runs, and the fact that he was accumulating too many miles per week. His total ignorance of my previous warnings had now left him in this somnolent supper condition. I figured that if he had followed my words of experience, he'd probably have been able to remain alert through the main course and capable of keeping his mashed potatoes at a safe silverware distance.

But no. Runners are often a stubborn lot, and he had fallen into that quicksand of muscle fatigue known as overtraining. I'd had the dubious distinction of being the North American champion of overtraining. I was the ignoramus of intensity, a multi-term president of the self-destructive running club.

I ran with the creed that overtraining was an oxymoron. Of course, I was the moron who operated under the mistaken belief that the feeling of continuously sore and tired legs meant training must be going quite well. I was the chief conductor on the train of strain, perilously plowing ahead on the railroad to ruin.

> **"I was the moron who operated under the mistaken belief that the feeling of continuously sore and tired legs meant training must be going quite well."**

As I looked across the dinner table at Mr. Potato Head, my glassy-eyed, overtrained running friend, I concluded that this condition was simply a runner's rite of passage. Something that needed to transpire or he'd go on to have some twisted and arrested development of running sensibility.

My personal awakening had occurred years earlier after running a race with some less-than-stellar results and lamenting my plight. A fellow runner mentioned to me that perhaps I'd been overshooting my ITT.

I attempted to fake knowledge for a minute or so at the totally unfamiliar term, but the best I could come up with for this acronym was *intellectually transparent tendencies.* I figured I was slightly off the mark. I finally conceded to a lack of knowledge and provided the proverbial "Say what?"

I was advised that this term meant individual training threshold. The apparently fine line between doing adequate training and going too far into that deep abyss of perpetual glycogen depletion.

I was quickly educated that perhaps I was running too much, too hard, too consistently. Ah, yes, I'd hit the overtraining trifecta—the Triple Crown of witlessness. I wasn't ready to admit anything and sarcastically replied, "Yeah, maybe if I'd only taken the last six months off with some periodic walking and nighttime ice-cream orgies, I'd have set a new PR. Hey, sleuth, I guess you uncovered my motto. Train harder, get slower. Live to loiter."

But deep down I knew there was truth to the advice about doing the overtraining gig and leaving no jig for the big dance. Perhaps I'd relied on some less-than-scientific principles in monitoring my training level of stress. Basically, if an impromptu nap had keeled me over into my keyboard by 10:00 A.M., and the emblem *qwertyuiop* was imprinted across my forehead, I'd conclude that quite conceivably I should have cut the run a couple miles short that morning. If my sudden visit into the sleep-cycle land of deep REMs went on longer than the time it took to complete my last marathon, and I uncovered more-than-ample drool emanating from my mouth upon awakening, well, perhaps one day off from running was in order. I guess I wasn't going to be confused with an exercise physiologist.

Once I became sufficiently armed with the concept of overtraining, I began to do a little more research into this phenomenon. I soon uncovered that there were indeed some more subtle signs of doing too much, other than beginning a run and realizing your shorts were still in your dresser drawer. Nothing like standing in the middle of the road in your birthday suit to assist with the conclusion that you might be a tad overfatigued.

In initially reviewing the signs of overtraining, I discovered I had what was termed a case of *the plods*. Apparently my general state of being carried with it all the symptoms of this lovely condition, including sore muscles, heavy legs, sluggishness, and a general feeling of fatigue and malaise. It was enlightening to learn that this was not the normal state of being for the average runner. I figured I just might be on to something here.

The first inquiry in a questionnaire regarding overtraining was, *Do you feel tired upon arising in the morning?* I thought that was pretty much a rhetorical question. Heck, wasn't that the definition of morning? I hadn't actually sprung out of bed with energy since Christmas morning in about 1964.

The questions continued with, *Does your normally comfortable pace leave you short of breath?* That inquiry left me amazed that one could actually experience something called a comfortable pace. I thought that was walking. I was beginning to conclude that perhaps something was a little askew in my constantly-gasping-for-breath training methodology. For me, an adequate training tempo run would put me into sufficient oxygen debt at the end that I didn't have the mental capacity to actually recall the course I'd just run. I was a repeat visitor to the land of lactic acid overload on an almost daily basis.

The next question was, *Do you experience any unusual muscle soreness?* I initially concluded this one was a negative, as my continuous state of muscle soreness was, by then, quite usual to me. I'm not sure I'd even recognize the feeling of walking down a flight of stairs without some discomfort. I realized that, perhaps, this just might be considered within the definition of *unusual.*

"Nothing like standing in the middle of the road in your birthday suit to assist with the conclusion that you might be a tad overfatigued."

Officially recognizing that I was deeply entrenched in the world of overtraining, I was pleased to learn that there was still hope. The key was backing off, slowing down, and making certain that hard training efforts were followed by one to two days of easy recovery runs. Before then, I'd always thought a recovery run amounted to jogging from my car into my house after driving back from a track workout.

Ultimately, like many runners before me, I learned how to properly train so that I wasn't consistently found peeling myself off my driveway at the end of training runs. My race times improved, as I began living the life beyond constant metabolic acidosis.

My mashed-potato-challenged friend also learned to take the long runs at an easy pace and to back off the miles the day before and after such an undertaking.

And, yes, like me, after a solid yet sensible training run, he can now make it well beyond dessert without exhaustion producing a sudden headlong leap into his plate. The many benefits of avoiding overtraining.

Chapter 27

The Idle Truth

My recent revelation might be aptly titled The Laziness of the Long Distance Runner. I have finally given in to the truth that I am part couch potato hiding within a well-conditioned body. I'm a running contradiction. I'm often an indolent individual who does intervals, a laggard who does long distance, a sluggard who does speed work. I am a runner and I am lazy.

I know that sounds like an oxymoron, but it's partly accurate. To paraphrase the philosopher Descartes, *I run, therefore I sit.* I suppose this puts me into quite a small and select group of runners. I'm one of the few, the not terribly proud, the slothful.

The fact is I've tried to deny the depth of my languor for as long as I've been a runner. I know the many positive effects that running can bring: better health, more self-confidence, enjoyment of the outdoors, etc. I had initially honed into the philosophy that running would give me this incredible reservoir of energy throughout the day to get everything accomplished. However, as I sat glued to my cushy chair and ottoman with television remote in hand after a Sunday morning 20-miler, there came a point at which it didn't do much good to deny the obvious.

Once the euphoria and adrenaline rush of a good run were over, I often returned to my roots of habitual inactivity. I could compete with the best of the non-runners in the area of lethargy. In my mind, though, it was clearly better to have run and been languid than to have never run at all.

I've convinced myself that the best method of recovery from a run is to remain immobile for as long as humanly possible. Suspended animation before and after a run is the key to my enjoyment of running. Everyone has a particular area of specialty, and I believe I've brought postrun idleness to new heights of expertise. The 1970s brought us the training benefits of LSD (long, slow distance) while I bring to the new millennium PSR (prolonged supine recovery).

> **"I've convinced myself that the best method of recovery from a run is to remain immobile for as long as humanly possible."**

I've further convinced myself that one of the reasons for my laziness is that it is a sacrifice I must make for the benefit of my running. My philosophy is that if I'm going to break my 10K PR in the near future, I've got to be sedentary as much as I can during my non-running time. I must look for every possible edge I can get. If that means buying a ranch house so that I can avoid the toll on my legs walking up and down stairs a couple of times a day, then so be it. If it means driving around for 15 minutes looking for that parking spot a little closer to my destination, I can do it. I may not have as much natural speed or endurance as my running competitors, but I have honed my ability to put my post-running training time to the greatest benefit. I can make the most of any opportunity for inaction.

They say the lazy really always want to do something. Well, I beg to differ. Once my run is complete I'm not looking to do anything. I've already done it. If I didn't run then I would be forced to admit some embarrassment at being as inert as I am at times. I have, without any terrible contrition, divided my day into two periods: running and dormancy. Since I run, I show no remorse for my extended fits of inactivity.

All right. Maybe I do exaggerate a wee bit. Perhaps I'm not quite as lazy as I've claimed, and I have slightly magnified things to make a point. But I do know that running allows me to enjoy my down time to a greater level. I am a runner first, lazy second. For me, these aren't mutually exclusive terms. Without one, I couldn't enjoy the other.

Those times my lawn grows a little too high or my driveway isn't shoveled—well, before my neighbors pass judgment on me, as they see me leisurely resting on my family room floor, I say, "Run eight miles of fartleks in my shoes."

In the meantime, could someone please get in here and pass me the remote?

Chapter 28

The Missing Drink

It was never anything I really consciously chose to avoid. But I started giving it a little more thought when I found myself waking up on the family room floor at 3:00 A.M., holding a half-eaten apple, with a little spittle rolling down the side of my face and wearing one of those *how did I get here* expressions.

This was usually about the time Suzanne Somers' voice would be blaring from the TV, imploring me to buy the latest version of the Thighmaster. In my sleepy stupor I'd find the phone and dial, but thankfully, I wasn't fully awake enough to remember my credit card number.

One night, as I crawled upstairs to bed, I had a thought. It is said that wisdom is good even if it comes late. With me, I'm just lucky when it comes at all. Having realized that life's day shift was to begin in a few hours, and fully recognizing that a morning run would maybe get me as far as the end of my driveway and back, I decided it was time to pull out all the stops.

My newly recruited alliance in the war against fatigue was something I really hadn't thought much about. I recalled having read some articles about the potential benefits it might have on running performance but it all seemed a little too complicated. Something about increasing lipolytic activity in the adipocyte, thereby enlarging the amount of free fatty acid oxidation in the plasma and decreasing the contractile threshold of a muscle, while sparing glycogen utilization. Yeah. Whatever.

But now was the time to give it a little more thought, since I needed an extra kick in my running shorts to get going. This seemed like the right juncture to explore the potential benefits of—drumroll, please—caffeine. They say that necessity is the mother of invention. This was more a case of lethargy being the father of a double espresso.

For those of you caffeine lovers wondering why I hadn't yet seen the coffee-pot light down at the old Maxwell House—well, I have the unique knack of eventually uncovering the obvious. And finally, at that time, I began to contemplate life with the Hills Brothers as my running partners.

The experts had always implored me to listen to my body. Well, I was finally hearkening to my own internal call. And it wasn't a nice, refreshing, soft chirp for smooth, cool spring water that I was hearing, but the clamorous shout for a brimming, full-bodied, hot jolt of java!

One day, before my morning run, I decided to give it a try and took a trip to the local coffeehouse. I figured I'd give it a full test for its impact on the normal whirlwind morning routine of breakfast for the children, cleanup, and so on, followed by a five-mile jaunt with the tandem running stroller.

Within 17 minutes of arriving back home, I'd fed and bathed both my boys, organized 20 years of running publications in chronological order and compiled an alphabetized list of leading articles, filled out online race applications for the next year's worth of races, cleaned the basement, reshingled the roof, and installed a sprinkler system for the backyard. For the brief moment I was stationary, my wife stared at me, baffled. I began to wonder whether the Deluxe Super Jumbo Mega Cup might have been a little too much in the way of my maiden caffeine cruise.

I next placed my children in the running stroller and we set off on one of our usual courses. As we effortlessly breezed up hills and sped along straightaways, I wondered whether I'd found an elixir. Had I stumbled upon the secret ingredient to the success of elite runners? Oh, sure, perhaps they trained twice a day, did some serious interval workouts, and ran 140 miles a week, but maybe it was this caffeine thing that truly got them cruising along at a sub-five-minute-mile pace. I began to speculate that sponsorships and endorsement deals might be in my future. Okay—maybe I was getting a little carried away by the quickness with which my synapses were snapping.

As I zoomed along the side of the road, setting personal training run records at each corner (while still possessing enough energy to incessantly talk to my running stroller passengers and point out each 10-yard landmark), I continued to contemplate that caffeine may be the answer. However, at that point my mind was moving at such warp speed to keep up with my hurtling body that I wasn't entirely certain anymore whether there was even a question. All that I could hear was a voice in my head sounding like Jack Nicholson in the movie *A Few Good Men*, shouting out, *You want energy? You can't handle the Vienna roast!*

"All that I could hear was a voice in my head sounding like Jack Nicholson in the movie *A Few Good Men*, shouting out, *You want energy? You can't handle the Vienna roast!*"

It turns out he was right. I think I initially overdid the old pep-and-vigor activator. I should have dipped slowly into the coffee stream rather than doing the complete caffeine plunge. The Energizer bunny now had nothing on me. After completing our run in world-record time, I felt more like Pepe the inexhaustible cheetah.

The fast pace of the morning continued on in much the same fashion throughout the remainder of the day. Good news was that I'd been able to complete all my tough running workouts for the next two weeks, and all job-related deadlines for the next nine months.

However, that night, I also found myself lying in bed with my eyes peeled wide open, my hands unconsciously tapping away on the blanket, and my feet dancing uncontrollably off the mattress to music from the VH1 weekly countdown. Guess I could have passed on the large can of Jolt at dinner and the two-liter bottle of Mountain Dew as a nighttime snack. I didn't take much solace from the fact I was awake to watch *Great Olympic Moments* on TV at 3:30 A.M.

As I was beginning to believe sleep was a poor substitute for caffeine, I pondered whether all this would improve my 10K or marathon time. I realized that doing the caffeine thing in the same gargantuan proportions for another day might keep me awake for the next 12 days. I also concluded that eventually my body would adjust to caffeine and the effect wouldn't be as great as it was that initial rocket-speed day.

I've since employed a little caffeine constraint. I save it for those special occasions such as mornings when I look down as I'm about to start a run, only to realize I've somehow bypassed that dressing stage where I actually change out of my pajamas.

It's then that I scurry back into the house and realize a little cup of joe might be of assistance to get the blood flowing a little quicker. If that doesn't work adequately, I then pull out all the stops. It's high time for that quadruple cappuccino and a quart of those chocolate-covered espresso beans!

Part VI

. . . .

The Marathon

Would We Be Doing Any of This if Pheidippides Had Been in Just a Little Better Shape?

Chapter 29

Marathon Madness

In looking back at the events of my first marathon, there is one word that quickly springs to mind. *Naïveté*. That's French for *Buddy, you didn't have a clue*. I'm quite amazed that all of it hasn't been obliterated from my memory.

One of my initial recollections would be my watch alarm going off promptly at 6:30 A.M. This only served to reveal the sheer depth of my ignorance. I admit to having operated under the ludicrous belief I'd actually get a normal night's sleep and that an alarm would be required to wake me up. I failed to appreciate how the twin cousins of anxiety and adrenaline would pay a nocturnal visit and keep my eyes prodded wide open.

I stored up on a grand total of 46 minutes of cumulative sleep for the night. I had my race number pinned on my shirt since 2:00 A.M. and had been to the bathroom 12 times since 4:00 A.M. (I wished I'd never read that last article on hydration, as I tried to memorize the exact location of every available port-a-john on the course).

I'd passed the hours by lathering my feet in about 13 coats of Vaseline since my arrival in the hotel room. I'd also spent my last few hours there trying, unsuccessfully, to get the chorus of "My

Sharona" stricken from the playback position of my memory bank (I shouldn't have started dial-surfing on the radio at 3:00 A.M.). It's not the kind of motivating music I envisioned drawing from at mile 21.

By 7:00 A.M. I decided to leave the womb of my hotel room and television set. The preceding 12 hours of bright-eyed confinement led me to conclude that time goes by painfully slowly when it's spent watching an infomercial of a combination juicer/stomach reducer/breadmaker/pasta maker/portable treadmill. The lack of coherent thought during this virtually sleepless night compelled me to purchase three of these all-in-one products. Go figure.

I began the half-mile walk to the starting line, all the while engaging in the profound internal debates of whether my shoelaces were too tight, singlet versus T-shirt, and whether I'd really done enough long training runs. The ever-present thoughts of a marathon man walking.

I placed myself near the sign that had my anticipated per-mile pace. Of course, I didn't have any real logical clue as to what my pace per mile should be. The combination of nerves and inadequate sleep led me to unconsciously do something I hadn't done since my high school gym class. I stretched. I tried, to no avail, to reacquaint my toes with my fingertips after a few years of distance between them. The attempted reunion stopped at my knees.

> "I began the half-mile walk to the starting line, all the while engaging in the profound internal debates of whether my shoelaces were too tight, singlet versus T-shirt, and whether I'd really done enough long training runs."

The announcer stated five minutes until the start, and I frantically glanced at the bathroom line that revealed my turn would arrive about the time the race winner crossed the finish line. Like a puppy dog with a full bladder, I began jumping in small circles as I tried to inconspicuously glance around for the nearest large tree. Or even a fire hydrant.

The starting gun eventually went off, followed instantaneously by the cacophony of countless beeps from the timers of runners' watches. The first mile marker arrived quickly and the split time provided me with good news and bad news. Good news was that I was 20 seconds ahead of my PR pace. The bad news was that I was 20 seconds ahead of my PR pace. Marathon myopia had officially begun.

I tried to slow down and realized I didn't have a firm grasp on the concept of pace. I had two speeds: all out or slow shuffle. Apparently, that in-the-middle thing must be called proper marathon pace. I attempted to convince myself that I was engaging in the racing tactic of elite runners. I was surging! Yeah, right. I was clueless.

I was doing everything to completely guarantee a rendezvous with that bastion of brutality otherwise known as the wall. Negative splits were clearly a concept I hadn't grasped. More like a banana split, as a relatively comfortable marathon was slipping away.

By seven miles I already found myself engaging in the mathematical Olympics of figuring out just what percentage of the 26 miles was then over. Like a runaway locomotive, I'd not yet gained the ability to slow down. I next surveyed the shoe attire of those runners surrounding me. I began to finally appreciate that my present running companions were clearly in a different league. I realized I was in the heretofore-uncharted territory (for me) of running with those in racing flats! I was a training-shoe interloper racing with the serious and talented cheetahs. It was then that I decided it was imperative that I ease back on the throttle.

Like clockwork, around 20 miles, I began to feel heaviness creep into my legs, as my stride became a trudge and I was, for all intents and purposes, exhausted. I don't mean tired like, *Gee, I'd better slow down a little to feel better.* If I'd tried to go any slower I'd be going backward. At that juncture, the last six miles appeared tantamount to doing the Western States 100.

This is where the prior euphoria of the race was now being mixed with reality and producing the lovely feeling of panic. I suddenly concluded I was pretty much marathon-illiterate. If ignorance were bliss, I should have been downright ecstatic.

But I couldn't quit. It wasn't so much about perseverance, completing a goal, or fighting through adversity. Truth was, there weren't any relief vehicles and my car was parked near the finishing line. The only way back was to proceed with my self-powered mode of transportation which at that juncture might have only generously labled dawdling.

> "By seven miles I already found myself engaging in the mathematical Olympics of figuring out just what percentage of the 26 miles was then over."

I moved forward and continued with my predilection for violating all rules of successful marathon running. I ignored aid stations for fear that, by stopping to drink, my legs would immediately take root and I'd never move again. I plodded on.

Ultimately, I crossed the finish line in sort of a slumberous shuffle as I searched for something to hold onto. The ground quickly became the most suitable option, as I simply sat down and did my best impression of a statue. I was supplied with food and drink, and I actually was resuscitated somewhat quickly, but at that point I considered staying awake an accomplishment. It was shortly thereafter that the mind warp that besets repeat marathoners crept into my conscience.

Apparently, in attempting to rid my body of lactic acid buildup, my short-term memory was being removed as well. I began to have strange thoughts. Visions of rhythmic running filled my head. Contemplation of my next marathon had already begun.

I was clearly afflicted with the

Madness of the Marathon Mind.

Chapter 30

From the Plains of Greece We Come

Just say the word with me. *Marathon.* To each of us it carries with it a certain emotion. Perhaps the euphoria (or is that delirium) of completion, or the admission that once was, quite frankly, more than enough. Or maybe the bliss of recognizing that your racing distance goes no further than a 10K and the only time you want to hit the wall is when you accidentally exit from the wrong side of the bed.

But no one can deny that the surge in popularity of the marathon race has had dramatic impact on the number of times the most inane question is asked by the non-runner. You know, the one you've patiently responded to countless times with the answer, "It'll be 26.2 miles—the same distance as the last one I ran," as your unathletic inquisitor responds, "Well, what are the odds that would happen! Exact same length, huh? Go figure!"

Though many of us know what it's like to run a marathon, not all of us know the history behind it. Perhaps you know that it has something to with a Greek battle, but maybe for all you know it might have been Phi Kappa Delta versus Sigma Nu. Well, I'm here to change all that. I'm the history professor in the microfleece tights and the reflective pullover. Let's begin today's lesson.

Legend has it that the first famous long-distance runner (well be-fore endorsement deals with shoe companies and guaranteed race-appearance fees) emerged from the plains of Marathon, Greece, in 490 B.C.

After the Athenians had defeated the Persians at the Battle of Mara-thon (which has a better ring than, say, the Battle of Dhidhimotikhonopolis—you'd be hard pressed to get that on a race T-shirt), the Greek warrior Pheidippides was chosen to bring the news of the great victory to the citizens of Athens. Problem was, the city was many, many miles off in the distance and the invention of the automobile or any form of mass transit was still a few years away.

So, young Pheidippides began running the approximately 26 miles from Marathon to Athens without the advantage of a big, carbo-loading pasta dinner the night before. He also ran without the ben-efit of aid stations, course volunteers, energy bars, bands playing music, or cheering spectators yelling, "You're looking great!" He also did not have the advantages of air-cushioned shoes, polyester shorts, or race directors at the finish line saying, "Here comes Mr. Pheidippides from Athens. Occupation is courier. Let's give him a nice round of applause!"

Pheidippides also fell victim to a common training blunder of mod-ern runners. Apparently he'd recently completed, in two days, a little jaunt of 150 miles to Sparta from Marathon in the effort to obtain some military assistance. Clearly, he'd failed to read the overtraining section from Herodotus' Book on Running, or he was simply trying to set a PR for a weekly mileage total.

Fact is, because of his recent ultra-event and his ongoing day job of warrior, he didn't allow himself sufficient rest before having to embark on his own marathon. (Of course, he had the better excuse of not actually knowing someone had preregistered him for the race.) He hit the proverbial wall around the large sign that read, six miles to Athens, and, tragically, he succumbed to exhaustion on the out-skirts of the city.

But all was not entirely lost as, in his last gasping and panting breath, he heroically uttered those final words of, "Rejoice, we con-quer! Got any sport drink?"

Tragically, it was then that the rigors of the marathon conquered him. For his tremendous effort he would become famous throughout the land. (Truth be known, Greek rumor has it that Pheidippides ran much farther than was necessary. Seems he got turned around slightly, and despite not having the benefit of an AAA TripTik, he chose to be the initiator of that time-honored male tradition—refusing to ask for directions. Then again, what challenge would a marathon be if Athens were really only 7 1/2 miles away?)

His legacy spawned the inclusion of the marathon race when the Olympics were inaugurated in Greece in 1896. Unfortunately, none of the 25 entrants seemed to have gained any lesson from the calamitous outcome of Pheidippides. The runners had pretty much no idea of what they were about to experience. A first-time marathoner encumbered with a healthy dose of naïveté is often not an attractive sight.

The participants all struggled to get to the finish line, and only nine actually completed the race. Due to their fatigue at the end, only four were even able to remember their names, and three of them were delirious enough to jump into the Olympic pool, thinking their next event was synchronized swimming. The good news was, in their derangement, they picked up a bronze medal for their impromptu pool performance.

As for the gold medalist in the inaugural Olympic marathon, the story is that a local Greek peasant named Spiridon Louis entered the Olympic Stadium first and slowly ran toward the finish line that was in front of the king's throne. (However, until I see actual photographs *of the finish, I still believe it was a Kenyan that won.) Allegedly, he was covered with dust and running in tattered, bedraggled, worn sandals (state-of-the-art, though). He would cross the finish line in 2 hours, 55 minutes, and 10 seconds for 40K, and his dazed smile was for realizing he'd now qualified for the Boston Marathon.*

His life would change forever. Everlasting glory was bestowed on him (once he passed the rigorous drug-screening laboratory) as the host country went ecstatic. He was given 25,000 francs (perhaps thereby becoming the first athlete to lose his amateur status), and was finally given permission by his future father-in-law to marry his longtime sweetheart (purportedly a bronze medalist in the badminton competition). Ah, the romance of running.

"A first-time marathoner encumbered with a healthy dose of naïveté is often not an attractive sight."

At the 1908 Olympics in London, the marathon distance was changed from 24.85 to 26 miles, to cover the ground from Windsor Castle to White City Stadium. You may then wonder, where did that lovely 385 yards get tacked on? It was added so that the race could finish in front of King Edward VII's royal box. Thus, the present 26.2-mile distance. And many a present-day marathoner wishes Windsor Castle were just a tad bit closer to the king's box when they find themselves doing the merciless march over the last mile of a marathon.

With its rising popularity, marathoners all have their unique stories about their races. I've been known to tell the one where I had a severe calf cramp from two miles on; encountered gale force winds of 60 miles per hour in whichever direction the run was heading; struggled through hail, snow, thunderstorms, and locusts at various times during the race; had a body temperature of 103 degrees and had just gotten over walking pneumonia; suffered bleeding feet from blisters halfway through the race; ran without aid stations, as the volunteers didn't show; couldn't see my split times because my contacts popped out at mile 3; had Montezuma's Revenge requiring 22 bathroom breaks; and had to run dramatically uphill at all times. Yet, despite all these obstacles, I persevered in the face of seemingly insurmountable adversity and set my PR by six minutes. It's my story and I'm sticking to it.

If any other runner tells you a similar, seemingly implausible story—well, you just nod your head approvingly, because you weren't there. For no matter what level of adversity a marathoner encountered, they did indeed achieve something that will change them forever.

Of course, not in the manner of Pheidippides and how his marathon tragically altered things. Imagine if only he'd said, "Hey, you, Deiopholese, I've got a bunion. How's about you running back to Athens to tell them the good news of our victory?"

But he didn't and, as they say, the rest is history.

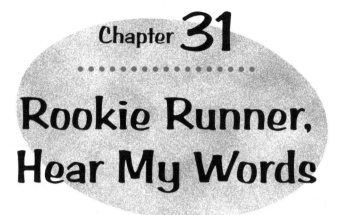

Chapter 31

Rookie Runner, Hear My Words

W here would we be without them? No, I don't mean light-weight, wind-and-water-resistant, microfiber fabric running suits, or the sweet aroma and taste of a good postrun recovery drink and carbohydrate-filled bar.

I mean those that truly keep the sport of running moving along in the race chute of life. Those that have the answer when we call, inquiring when the latest lightweight, three-ounce, slipper-like fluorescent shoe with width sizing, no laces, and a pedometer inserted in the sole will be available.

Those that, year after year, sponsor the runs, bribe for race volunteers, sometimes lose money on race T-shirts, and keep their patience with those that view the postrace refreshment table as an opportunity to stockpile their refrigerator for the next month and a half.

Thank you, Mr. and Ms. Running Store Owner! This sport drink is for you!

Thanks for giving the package discount on the case of running socks. Thank you for organizing the weekly speed workout (although on that last repeat mile, one might feel a tad masochistic in actually thanking you for the torment). Thanks for keeping the shelves well-stocked with energy gels and allowing us to stand in the back of your store and bask in the glow of a colorful array of race applications. And thanks for having a complete library of running-related books and magazines for those of us junkies who have long since abandoned all other forms of reading material as unworthy.

But, most importantly, there are those that must thank you for molding them from a jumbo-size, out-of-condition, overweight, uncoordinated bundle of atrophied muscle mass to a sleek, smooth, agile racing machine.

For you are the architect of the athlete, the converter of the couch potato, the transformer of the torpid. Most importantly, you are the molder of marathoners—the training class instructor. We salute you with our polyester, breathable, aerodynamic hats!

Multitudes of runners have you to thank for leading them into the Promised Land of marathon race day. A place where they can experience the lovely togetherness and camaraderie of being sandwiched side by side with 20,000 strangers, all of whom nervously wait for the start while contemplating whether one last trip to the port-a-john is feasible.

As you motivate runners to racers, it ultimately comes time to provide them with the Ten Commandments of Racing from Mt. Stamina. The commandments of racing that can only be presented through the omniscient words of the local running store marathon coach. The story unfolds as follows:

In the fifth month of training, rookie runners and their local running store coach venture out to the wonderful, exciting world of the mega-entrant marathon. As their bus drops them off near the starting line of the 26.2-mile event, neophyte runners anxiously stretch on the ground while the running store coach calls out to them from the lush and green grassy hill above them.

The running store coach says, "I can only assume everyone has listened well to me these last five months. I have guided you, instructed you, and transformed you. I've brought some of you out from the land of idleness, from the house of sloth.

"Now, you are all embarking on a world that cannot be adequately described in words, but only through experience. You will be entering an extraordinary land, filled with new and tempting electrolyte replacement drinks and aid stations with enchanting treats. A land with a multitude of runners running a fast pace, and a course with a slight downhill grade for the first four miles.

"It will be seen as the land of enticement. A land of easily bettering the goal time we have presently set for each of you. Hear me, my runners! You must not be led into this straight-away of temptation! You must adhere to our strategy, for I speak to you now as the voice of experience."

The running coach goes on, "If, within the marathon race, you stay on target with your planned pace, if you replenish yourself with familiar liquids at the appropriate aid stations, if you take in the energy gels at the designated miles, and stay focused on our agreed-upon approach, then you shall enjoy this potentially majestic and marvelous marathon experience.

"However, if you do otherwise, you will undoubtedly find yourself wandering mindlessly in the rigorous land of mara-thon mania, at the painful Wall of Depletion. It is not a pretty picture. And never let it be said that I didn't warn you."

The running store coach stares at the runners for emphasis of his words and then raises his hands high in the air. Looking at the flock of neophyte runners, he then speaks again, "These will be the final and most important words of guidance. For these will be the Ten Commandments of Racing. You must hear my words and observe my remarks, my athletes."

1 You shall have no coaches besides me. Don't be tempted by what others may now tell you of rest walks, of com-bating blisters, of achieving negative splits, of lengthening your stride, or of eliminating sideaches. I am your sole tutor in poly-ester tights. You shall follow all that I have taught you so that you may live to comfortably run today and on days to come.

2 You shall not look around you and covet your fellow racer's multicolored, wick-away-moisture singlet, matching shorts, racing shoes, polycarbonate nonslip-nose-piece sunglasses, running watch with ergonomically designed buttons, blister-free socks, or perspiration-wicking running hat. By the way, all those items will be 10 percent off in the weeks to come.

3 You shall not wrongfully assume a place or position in the starting line area that is not reflective of your estimated and appropriate pace per mile. To do so would be to take a deserved spot from a fellow runner and place you in the horrifying position of becoming instant roadkill when the starting gun fires. Shame on you!

4 You shall try to dispose of your drink cups, food wrappers, Band-Aid packaging, petroleum jelly tubes, Breathe-Right strips, and anti-inflammatory pill containers in the appropriate depositories, and stay in tune with the endurance of your bladder so as to avoid creating an impromptu restroom.

5 You shall not lose your poise or lose sight of your expected pace because of the excitement and adrenaline rush of the race. For to do so would assure you a rendezvous in the unforgiving valley of exhaustion, where darkness and discomfort shall follow you for all the miles of your race, and you will dwell in the house of agony for what seems like forever.

6 If you should feel depleted, you shall nonetheless enthusiastically, resolutely, and merrily proceed with smiling, forward movement at all times, for you are wearing my store's name on your race singlet.

7 You shall applaud and encourage your fellow companions in commitment. Share your drink at the aid station, your space on the road, your postrace refreshments. Step delicately over those who crash before you, for they did not have the guidance I provide. And never show disrespect by misrepresenting your finish time to another runner.

8 You shall not elbow, push, poke, trip, cut in front of, jostle, run too close behind, shove, or step on the foot of any other runner you encounter in the land of racing. Nor shall you spit, hurl, blow, throw up, or toss any bodily product to any place other than the side of the road.

9 You shall not use excuses for a race performance beneath your expectations, including too much wind, too hot, limited course port-a-johns, too many hills, chafing, indigestion, inadequate carbo-loading, aid station lines, cramps, or inaccurate split times. Most importantly, you will never, ever, ever, ever blame your coach. That would be heresy.

10 You shall give thanks, as you will ultimately cross the finish line. You will slowly move forward on shaky legs as you perform the lactic acid shuffle. You must not forget to give appreciation to the race director, volunteers, and sponsors, for they are your providers. Without them we are alone, wandering aimlessly, looking for organized competition, and without a T-shirt collection.

The neophyte runners, in unison, enthusiastically raise their water bottles in assent and collectively yell, "Amen, Obi Wan Aerobe!"

They are acknowledging that they've heard everything from their leader and will obey the commandments of racing.

And with that agreement, neophyte racers and running coach walk slowly together to the starting line and into an exciting and exhilarating new arena.

For they have seen the light, in the wondrous world of racing.

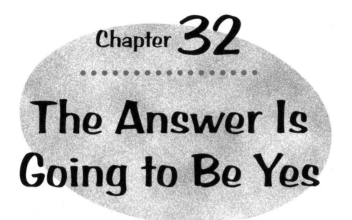

Chapter 32

The Answer Is Going to Be Yes

I t doesn't matter how many marathons I've run or how fast I've run them; it always seems to come back to the same lingering question. As constant as my always sending my race application in after the late registration fee goes into effect, whenever someone learns that I am a runner, the next words I routinely hear are, "Well, big fella, have you run the New York City Marathon?"

Such is the mind-set of the general public, given that the race has become such an icon of popular culture. You run with the bulls in Pamplona and with the world at the NYC Marathon. Without question, the Boston Marathon has incredible tradition, character, stature, and mystique. Where else can you have the lovely anaerobic thrill of going up Heartbreak Hill while feeling like you're being passed by slow moving spectators. For over one hundred years, Boston has taken marathoners through the hills of Newton and the downhill to the finish line on Boylston Street where you can only hope your quadriceps are still functioning. Achieving a qualifying time for Boston is the pinnacle of running for many marathoners.

There's also the size and pancake-flat course at the LaSalle Bank Chicago Marathon and the lovely musical entertainment of the

Suzuki Rock n' Roll Marathon in San Diego. All are extraordinary races that provide unbelievable memories. But New York City is distinct.

The closest I'd gotten to running up the middle of Fifth Avenue, unconcerned about getting run over by a taxi, was seeing it on television. I'd read of the ingenuity of Fred Lebow. I knew about the consistency of eight-time winner Greta Waitz, the classic 1983 duel between Geoff Smith and Rod Dixon, the wins of John Kagwe, the epidemic and festive community spirit, the five bridges and boroughs, and the ethnic neighborhoods.

> "**S**omehow, I hadn't truly felt the complete aura and enveloping experience of marathon running until I completed the big kahuna—the New York City Marathon."

Nonetheless, as if I were confessing to some appalling running faux pas, I'd have to meekly respond, "Well, uh, no, I haven't actually run that one yet."

I'd receive a slightly unimpressed look from my questioner and a disapproving and dismissive "Oh. I see."

I'd immediately pipe up, "Whoa, buddy. I ran a 50-mile race once at altitude you've only seen in a plane! I've competed in more marathons than the number of cumulative miles you've run in your life! I burn off more calories before 6:00 A.M. than you do in a month! Am I not worthy because I haven't graduated from the school of New York City Marathon running?" To some, apparently not.

My other running accomplishments were viewed as no more than a chopped liver sandwich at the Carnegie Deli. Somehow, I hadn't truly felt the complete aura and enveloping experience of marathon running until I completed the big kahuna–the NYC Marathon.

Well, finally, this was going to be my year. I'd get that running monkey off my hamstrings. If I ever found myself running in France, and that old persistent question popped up, my answer could at last be a resounding and emphatic *"Ah, mais oui! Oui!"*

I'd be able to say I'd moved with a zillion human centipedes across the Verazanno-Narrows Bridge, sipped Gatorade in Brooklyn, sauntered to rap music in Bedford-Stuyvesant, and felt the warmth of the Hasidic Jews in Williamsburg and the Poles in Greenpoint. I'd have hummed the "59th Street Bridge Song" gliding across the Queensboro, been virtually bowled over by the thunderous roar of the crowd entering Manhattan, and high-fived spectators in Harlem. I'd be able to nonchalantly respond with a look of *Been there. Done that.*

As I eagerly sent for my application I could hear Frank Sinatra singing,

> *"Start spreading the news, I'll be there race day, New York, New York!*
> *These old running shoes are joining the fray, right through the very sole of them, New York, New York!*
> *If I can get accepted there, I can get in anywhere.*
> *It's up to me, New York, New York!"*

I quickly realized the tenacity, perseverance, and pacing of a runner all began with the detailed NYC application process which was in effect at that time. Gratefully, I ultimately got in, and was given the wonderful opportunity to experience a side stitch on the Pulaski Bridge, develop a toe blister in the Bronx, fight my way through glycogen depletion down Fifth Avenue, and have my trapezius muscles tighten like a vise down around Marcus Garvey Park.

I got the wonderful privilege of having my quadriceps feel like overcooked macaroni on the hills of Central Park and of ultimately achieving the pleasure of total exhaustion at Tavern on the Green. Well, perhaps only marathoners can truly appreciate *that* profound attraction. It's like the great Czech Republic runner and triple gold medalist Emil Zatopeck once said,

> "*If you want to run, then run a mile. If you want to experience another life, run a marathon.*"

That's it. What better place to experience another life than in a city that is often described as another world? An energetic city that truly is where the world comes to run. On race day, the Statute of Liberty inscription should read:

> *Give me your taut calf muscles, your powerful lungs, your multi-national masses craving to run 26.2 miles. Send these, the marathoners, and we'll lift our open arms, ferociously applaud your effort, and show you the time of your life.*

Down the road, if I ever ran in Spain and that universal query popped up, I'd enthusiastically respond, *"Si. Corri el maraton de la ciudad de Nueva York!"*

Here I come, sponge station at 18.5 miles! I'm on my way to the joy of lactic acid buildup in the Big Apple!

> *Post Script: On November 7, 1999, I rode the 5:30 A.M. bus to Staten Island; had bagels and coffee with runners from all over the world; set a PR for time spent waiting for the port-o-john; experienced the organizational genius of the race directors; shared a New York Times newspaper with a woman from Germany; provided a prophylactic blister Band-Aid to a man from Colombia; and ran the entire course about 10 yards behind a gentleman wearing a singlet with the word Venezuela*

across the front and back. And now, like Pavlov's dog, anytime the words **New York City Marathon** *are uttered, I immediately hear the sounds that were shouted out, in front of me, about 589 times throughout the race from the enthusiastic spectators: "Go, Venezuela!" I guess that's a little more rhythmic to hear than cheers for someone wearing a T-shirt advertising her city's name of Yamatokoriyama.*

It was all it was cracked up to be. And, go ahead, ask me that universal query again. I'm ready. New York City Marathon? Of course. Piece of cake.

Chapter 33

Coach Rod and the Zone

A strange thing happened when I waited for the beginning of my second marathon. While engaging in my prerace routine of contemplating stretching, for some inexplicable reason, I began seeing and hearing Rod Serling of *Twilight Zone* fame.

My initial thought was that I was about to have a breakthrough race. With this odd transcendental encounter, I was experiencing a runner's high and the race hadn't even started! This was fantastic!

But it wasn't. I focused on the voice and noted that he wasn't reciting the normal introduction to his old television show. Zeroing in on the words that were reverberating from my head to my then-trembling knees, I realized that, in his distinctive cadence, Mr. Serling was warning me of my return visit to the land of debilitation.

My one previous marathon was not the rhythmic ride and smooth-flowing stream I had hoped for. From what I could actually recall, it was more a ragged and rough tumble, which had the less-than-placid flow of a deluge of water plowing into a dam.

With trepidation running rampant in my legs, I had to listen to this one-man-welcome-wagon race director offer the following not-so-uplifting words of wisdom:

You're about to enter another dimension.
A dimension not only of enervation but also glycogen depletion.
It may actually feel that your quadriceps are about to explode.

It's a dimension where your pace suddenly slows dramatically,
Where energy is but a distant recollection.
Where your arms feel like overweight dumbbells,
And mile markers seem to come much more slowly.

It's a return engagement into forgotten territory.
It will feel like you're moving backwards.
It's nothing your memory allowed you to fully remember,
As your mind has been engaging in selective recall.

You recollect the euphoria and relief.
Crossing the finish line can still be envisioned.
This final joy remains the prominent detail.
You've forgotten the more arduous trial of character.

You're about to re-enter the region of weariness,
Your past will once again be your present.
A return rendezvous to a former dimension.
Why are you even here?

Welcome to the depths of your fears.
You thought things were all right, but—
You'll soon be seeing the 20-mile signpost up ahead.
Your next stop, the Exhaustion Zone!

Terror quickly set in. I felt a little queasy, as beads of sweat started forming on my brow and my hands began to tremble. The only sound I could discern was my newly appointed and self-anointed Coach Serling, smugly chuckling to himself. I wasn't overly amused.

This wasn't exactly the prerace warm-up I'd envisioned. This Serling guy sure had a way of bringing out a lovely sense of alarm.

My initial euphoria for the beginning of the race was quickly being mixed with the reality of the moment; the product was sheer anxiety.

The soliloquy of my *Twilight Zone* partner was echoing in my head. I was slowly succumbing to the reality of the words coming from this chain-smoking, science-fiction television writer.

I gulped. I attempted to redirect my focus and took a quick trip down the memory lane of my last five months of solid training. Things were different this time. Even so, I knew that the physical debilitation he'd serenaded me about was the worst that could happen. And I'd survived that before! I think.

My runner's resolve reappeared. I was experienced. I blurted out, "You can't scare me, Mr. Serling! No sirree! I'm on to you, Mr. Sunshine Face!" My fellow runners began taking a few steps away from me and wondering whether I'd overloaded on my carbo-load or eaten the petroleum jelly instead of spreading it on my feet.

I thought, *Rod, old buddy, this is what I live for. This is why I laced 'em up.* I wasn't a neophyte. I had one marathon in my shorts and I was ready for another. *Submit that for your perusal! You don't scare me, Mr. Charisma!*

I then exclaimed, in kind of a primal scream, "I'll see you on the finish side. There ain't no stopping me now. Dimensions, shmensions! Whatever. You can't spook me. This ain't no Halloween Trick-or-Trot run, fella. Now go on and get out of here!"

Mr. Serling, my inimitable master of ceremonies, couldn't shake me. I was ready for all that was ahead. I welcomed it like an old friend. I scoffed at his attempted voice of reason. I ignored his endeavor to question my sanity. I cast him aside like an old, worn-out racing T-shirt, as I enthusiastically walked to the starting line.

Then I caught his face out of the corner of my eye. Mr. Serling gave me a smile and a well-designed wink. What the heck was going on here? It suddenly dawned on me. He was on my side. This had been reverse psychology at its finest. He'd provided a masterful job of psyching me up! Apparently, he could write about Martians as well as coach marathons. He was part Bill Bowerman, part Vince Lombardi, and part Stephen King. You got me, Mr. Serling. Big time. I was under his captivating spell.

We exchanged a thumbs-up sign and off I went. With excitement. With eager anticipation. Into the Exhaustion Zone. A universe of possibilities.

I was ready to be taken to another dimension! Bring me to that middle ground between start and finish, between well-stocked stores of energy and depletion, between lengthy strides and a more shortened shuffle. Not *Twilight Zone's* land of imagination, but a runner's welcome reality!

I thought, *Thanks, Coach.* Then it hit me. Maybe I should have gotten his expert insight on the speed and duration of my tempo-training runs. He might know something about that also.

Part **VII**

· · · · · · · · · · · ·

Injuries

What Tunes Does the
Iliotibial Band Play?

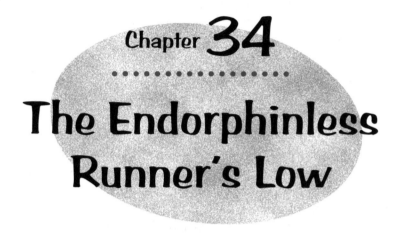

Chapter 34

The Endorphinless Runner's Low

I've been fairly lucky throughout my running years (knock on the bottle of anti-inflammatories) that I've been able to avoid a major injury. You know, the one that turns a suddenly sidelined runner into a foaming Neanderthal because he can't get his daily dosage of endorphins.

Unfortunately, I recently became part of that contemptible club, with the required entry being one or more consecutive months off from running because of an injury. I wish I had some battle-produced reason like having suffered a stress fracture in my foot after running 180 miles per week for 10 consecutive weeks, or having injured my Achilles tendon on my 74th consecutive 400-meter repeat. That would have gotten a "Whoa, Nellie!" but, alas, my reason gets a "Yo, idiot."

My less-than-awe-invoking excuse was to pull a hamstring playing basketball. I know. What's a runner doing playing with those weekend warriors who are otherwise known as the gang of anterior-cruciate-ligament-tears-waiting-to-happen?

The truth is that I've always played basketball, despite the fact long-distance runners usually can't jump up to the curb even with a sprinting start. I'm lucky if when I "sky," someone is able to insert a 3 x 5 card under my Air Jordans. I mean the flat way. Not vertical. Just like me. My scouting report would read, *Great stamina, no spring.*

I'd been able to avoid a basketball-related injury, other than having my shot ferociously blocked and the word *Spalding* tattooed across my forehead, while my opponent cried out, "Take that, Marathon Boy!"

The problem with being wounded was that I quickly realized I'm not the Joan-Benoit-Samuelson-type of injured runner. She underwent knee surgery shortly before the 1984 Olympic Trials and had a stationary bicycle rolled into her hospital room to maintain her conditioning.

On the other side of the cross-training room, I wheeled the refrigerator into my bedroom, made sure new batteries were in the television remote control, programmed the number of the pizza delivery store into my speed dial, and began to do my best Brian Wilson imitation while I perfected my sulking. It felt like I doubled my weight within the first six hours of the conclusion that a sedentary lifestyle was on my agenda for the next few weeks.

Despite watching all of Leslie Nielsen's movies, I was able to keep my mental abilities attuned enough to reach some halfway intelligent observations about being on the injured list. Specifically, not being able to run produces Injured Runners Saving Time, wherein days seem to triple in length. This did allow me to watch ESPN's *Running and Racing* without having to set my VCR to 1:00 A.M., and those 3:00 A.M. infomercials can actually be interesting when the only other thing on is the gripping account of the history of the American fruit fly on the educational channel.

Also, your laundry is cut in half, but showers don't feel nearly as rewarding when they're post-repose as opposed to post-run.

Having recently resumed my running, I've discovered a critical piece of information. It's best to refine your *I can run across the street before that car comes* internal tracking system. Not being in as great a condition as pre-injury tends to make the cars appear to come toward you a heck of a lot quicker. Discretion is the better part of becoming a hood ornament.

I also discovered that, in addition to the funny bone, there is a funny muscle. Otherwise known as the famous comedic trio of Misters Semitendinosus, Semimembranosus, and Biceps Femoris. The Three Stooges of the fibrous tissue world. These hamstring muscles come with their own warped sense of humor by providing absolutely no pain until I was three miles away from home during my first post-injury run. As I hobbled home, they sent me the not-so-subtle message that one more week of coconut cream candies on the couch would have been a better idea.

As I walked home looking like the poster child for impetuous re-injured runners, I realized my lack of fresh oxygen over the prior month was also producing certain demented delusions. My hallucinogenic state, produced by a lack of exercise, enabled me to believe I was actually hearing a little mocking laughter coming from the back of my left leg. The haranguing snicker of the hamstring that was presently in complete control of every aspect of my life. My theory is that these flights of phantasms were the direct product of a lack of perspiration. Kind of a reverse runner's high.

Ultimately, I healed and did make it back onto the roads. I realized there's life post-injury and post-*Naked Gun* movies. For Leslie Nielsen and me.

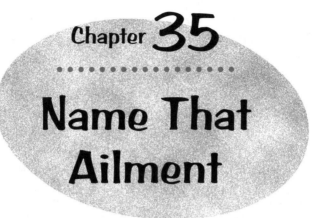

Chapter 35

Name That Ailment

W hat a new runner truly needs most is not necessarily a great-fitting orthotic, the knowledge not to wear all-cotton socks, or even a singlet that doesn't chafe under the armpits. Rather, before one should even think about basking in the glory of running a mile for the first time, or the inherent joy of a sweat-soaked T-shirt, one needs to be completely versed on the subject of running injuries. Hey, a meter of prevention is worth a 5K of cure.

I realize that running is considered a non-contact sport (excluding some winter mornings when my feet's internal radar abilities find any patch of sidewalk ice resulting in a derriere glide into the nearest snowbank), but running can indeed produce injuries from overuse, misuse, or just being generally obtuse.

To prevent a two-day injury from progressing into a month-long layoff, a new runner needs to possess the knowledge that would enable him to be a successful contestant on the game show *Name That Running Ailment*. The game show preference among the endorphin-loving crowd. The show designed to entertain as well as educate, which would go something like this:

The oversized Gore-Tex drapes begin to open slowly as a voice from off stage provides the welcoming statement, "Let's introduce the host of our show, Dr. Cy Attica!" The talented Iliotibial Band plays the theme song, "Long May You Run," by Neil Young.

Dr. Cy Attica stands center stage, neatly attired in a lightweight, long-sleeve, nylon running top, reflective hat, and relaxed-fit black fleece tights. He has sunglasses propped on the top of his head, a whistle around his neck, and a clipboard in his hand as he welcomes the audience. "Thank you, and welcome to another edition of *Name That Running Ailment*. The only game show where you are not only able to win money and fabulous prizes, but also learn valuable tips to avoid and identify running injuries.

"Our first contestant, Larry York, is a reformed smoker whose previous idea of exercise was weeding his garden twice a year and walking the daily 100 yards from his parking spot to his office. Now he's training to run his first 5K and has lost 30 pounds. Let's give him a nice round of applause. He'll have his work cut out in going up against one of our faster contestants, our returning champion, Joe Drew, a former Olympic-Marathon qualifier!

"A little course refresher for our audience: I'll begin the game by providing the number of letters in the mystery ailment. When it is a contestant's turn, he will spin the giant stopwatch, which has different race distances listed on it. The stopwatch will randomly stop at a race distance, which, when multiplied by 100, reflects the amount of money available to win if he guesses a correct letter.

"Remember to speak clearly into the oversized squirt bottle, which acts as your microphone. When you think you know the answer, just push down on the large computer racing chip in front of you and state your ailment. The winner may use his money to shop in our in-studio running store.

"Unfortunately, as our audience knows, if you lose, you will not only forfeit your money, but you will also be required to experience the ailment in question for a short time, in our famous First-Aid-Tent Virtual Injury Chamber.

"Those who tuned in the other night will recall that a nasty plantar's fasciitis injury caused a wee bit of discomfort for our losing contestant. And need I remind anyone of last week's champion, who was eventually required to demonstrate the old black-toenail

malady? To his credit, our dedicated audience now knows this is caused by a pooling of blood under the toenail as a result of the toe rubbing or hitting the top of the shoe! We educate and entertain, so let's play!

"Now, remember, these curable ailments are not limited to runners, but they are known to occur with runners. All right! Our first condition tonight is two words and has 18 letters. Our new contestant will go first. Audience, let's give him the famous initial command on Name That Running Ailment."

The audience, in unison, slowly and enthusiastically screams, "Spin that stopwatch!"

Larry spins the watch and it lands on 10K, which means he's going for $1,000. Larry exclaims, "How about the letter A?"

"We happen to have one A," *replies Dr. Cy Attica.*

The lovely physician's assistant, Miss Anne T. Inflammatory, turns over the first letter of the two-word ailment that the contestants are attempting to solve.

"For $100, I'd like to buy a symptom," *proclaims Larry.*

Dr. Cy Attica grabs a race entry form from his clipboard, which also contains a list of the various symptoms involved with the ailment. "All right, the first symptom clue is that this condition involves pain along the area connecting the gastrocnemius to the soleus. Any guesses?"

Larry responds, "Hey, I'm just a running rookie. I barely know my bunions from my corns, so no guesses here."

Joe spins the stopwatch with the look of a seasoned veteran who knows his tarsal tunnel from his carpal tunnel and his DOMS from his RICE. The stopwatch comes to a halt on the marathon marker and thus the turn is worth $2,620. With great confidence, Joe guesses the letter I, and Anne T. Inflammatory turns over the fourth letter of the first word and the fifth, seventh, and ninth letter of the second word.

"All right, Mr. 2:21:00 Marathoner, any guesses?"

With a smug look, Joe responds, "Well, I know this one from having had it during the spring of 1997. How about that bothersome injury named after a Greek warrior who, as a baby, was held by his ankle and dipped in the magical pond by his mother? His only area of potential harm was his heel, where he would later be hit and injured by an arrow. How about that old nemesis, Achilles tendinitis?"

"Whoa, Mr. Speed Machine, that is much more than we need, but it's positively correct! Looks like you gained more than a little familiarity with this condition," replies Dr. Cy Attica.

The audience applauds wildly as they wave their souvenir headbands, nasal strips, and energy gel packets.

"For our studio audience and those watching at home, Achilles tendinitis is caused by inflammation of the Achilles tendon, and it is often caused by tired or fatigued calf muscles that cause the Achilles to bear too much of the running stress. For $100 in bonus money, can you tell me which bone the bulk of this tendon is attached to?"

"Would that be the calcaneus?"

"That's right again," replies Dr. Cy Attica. "Very impressive even for a veteran runner. Amazing! You'll now have $2,720 to spend in our in-house running store and, as our rules state, you'll have the length of time to shop that is equal to the average mile pace for your best 5K. But first, Mr. Road Runner, for $1,000 in bonus money, name five recommended running surfaces to use to avoid running injuries.

"As you contemplate that one, let's thank Larry for playing, but unfortunately, Larry, you must now spend 15 minutes in the First-Aid-Tent Virtual Injury Chamber where you'll experience the symptoms of Achilles tendinitis. Larry, you'll be assisting those in our studio audience and at home to gain an even greater understanding of this condition as you can point out the area of discomfort as well as where ice should be placed to treat the inflammation. You'll also be able to demonstrate some stretching exercises to help with the condition. Let's first thank Larry for the sacrifice he'll be making for the greater education of runners everywhere!

"And as consolation prizes, we'll provide Larry with an Achilles tendon stretcher in case this injury ever does actually occur to him outside our little virtual world. We'll also throw in a guaranteed entry spot in next year's Walt Disney World Marathon. That will give you some training incentive!

"But first, back to Joe. Can you answer the bonus question?"

Joe replies, "How about sand, grass, dirt trails, tracks, and cinder paths?"

"*That is correct! And while you jog over to our in-studio store, and I escort Larry down our indoor track straightaway to the Virtual In-jury Chamber, everyone can look at our giant video screen. There you will see a demonstration of how to treat fluid accumulation be-tween the skin's inner and outer layer because of excess friction—often known as that unwelcome visitor at the 20-mile mark of a marathon, the king of inconvenience, Sir Blister.*

"*And now, if the band could play 'In the Long Run' by the Eagles, while everyone watches Larry and Joe on the large split screen in their respective on-stage locations, I'll say so long and see you for our next injury.*

"*For now, this is Dr. Cy Attica, wishing you and yours good run-ning and good diagnosis.*"

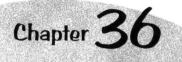

Chapter 36

Run to Glory, or at Least the End of the Block

Like the swallows returning to San Juan Capistrano, California, each March, and like the buzzards returning to Hinkley, Ohio, before April, I seem to have my own annual event. A little less migratory and a lot more annoying.

For the last few years, like some strange and twisted biological cycle, at some point in January or February, I will pull a muscle. Or a tendon. Or strain a ligament. I'm an equal-opportunity connective-tissue abuser.

It's never anything overly serious and soon enough I'm healed. I realize that there are some runners who view a sidelining injury as an opportunity for personal growth, self-discovery, and a chance to channel their harnessed energy down cerebral vistas. To this I say, "Hasta la vista." If I'd have wanted to study famous Norwegian existential songwriters of the mid-15th century—well, I'd have found the time by now. I'm slightly less scholarly, as I'll spend my daily running time coming up with catchy jingles and other forms of poetry to describe my maladies. I'm a wee bit embarrassed to admit how many missed running days it took me to finally come up with this: "Sometime during winter, and definitely before spring, it seems almost inevitable that I will pull my hamstring." There's apparently an inverse relationship between consecutive non-running days and my ingenuity. It was a solid month before this limerick finally kicked in:

There was a runner from the Midwest,
Who always tried to do his best.
He would train all year round,
Except when a pulled muscle did abound,
And then he'd give his gluteus maximus a rest.

I'll always remember January of 1998 for this lovely ditty: "It's not something over which to scream and fuss, but running on an indoor track led me to pull my latissimus dorsus." Hey, some injured runners may wish to spend their extra time learning how to wire their bathrooms with surround-sound speakers or cook gourmet, vegetarian, low-cholesterol, wheat-free Armenian appetizers. Instead, I've got my poetry priorities. I must admit that healing did arrive before I could ever come up with a haiku about my vastus lateralis. But February 4th to 17th, 1999, will always be remembered for a sweet, sentimental poem regarding my gastrocnemius. I'm already ahead of the poetic injury game, as I've nearly completed a nice little quatrain about my Achilles tendon and it hasn't even been injured yet.

Groundhog Day has a different meaning for me. My prognosticating anatomy tells me if I've got a slight muscular injury by February 2, then I'll still have time to recover and make the four-mile St. Patrick's Day race in mid-March. After February 2, and I'm looking at nothing sooner than the Easter Bunny Bop 5K.

Most runners have a two-pronged approach to a possible injury. The first is, if I ignore it long enough it will go away. Otherwise known as the infamous *I can run through it* theory, and formally recognized as the Mindset of the Myopic Runner.

This unreasonable approach is usually followed by a layoff of a few weeks and the newly found creed of being much smarter next time. This attitude will, inevitably, last until—drum roll, please—the *next time*. Like those migratory swallows, most runners return to that former and quite ineffective *run through it* philosophy. Live and learn? More like run and disregard.

This repetitive pattern is a common malady for which there is no known cure, and research has established there's a direct correlation between one's best 10K time and the degree of myopia.

Returning from an injury-produced layoff will lead one to the *comeback*. There are fewer real comebacks in sports these days because the time out for injury has been decreased by more effective methods of treatment. I don't think it'll be long before we hear a sports announcer saying, "Word from the dressing room is that he's torn his anterior cruciate ligament but is now undergoing some arthroscopic surgery with a graft from a cadaver. He'll rehab at halftime and should be back at full strength by the middle of the third quarter."

For one who has the patience of a hyperactive puppy, comebacks are the most difficult part of running for me. I want results and I want them yesterday. Experience has allowed me to calculate my own formula for returning from an injury and determining how much and how often I should be running. Some may adhere to the 10-percent rule, which is that you shouldn't increase your weekly mileage beyond that amount or risk injury. The problem I discovered with this formula was, since my initial post-injury runs could be measured in yards and my pace timed with a sundial, applying the 10-percent rule enabled me to conclude I'd be in marathon shape somewhere in the year 2078. I'm not that patient.

Thus, my recommended formula is that you need to take your average weekly mileage for the five weeks preceding your injury; divide it by five or by the number of pounds you've gained during your layoff, whichever is greater; multiply that by the number of running magazines you subscribe to; add the total number of running shoes you presently rotate; subtract half the number of races you ran in the preceding 10 months, excluding December through March; and add five if you can correctly spell *Khalid Khannouchi* and *Naoko Takahashi* on the first attempt. This is the number of miles you should run in your first week back from injury. Subsequently, increase the number of miles per week by the number of old race numbers from the last two years that presently reside in your home. Add seven if any of those were PRs, and three if you own racing flats.

I'm optimistic that my yearly string of pulled muscles will eventually come to an end. Perhaps that will occur when I finally employ some of the things I've read about to avoid injury. Maybe the last limerick could be:

> *There was a runner who thought he'd found the key,*
> *From annual layoff where his body would atrophy.*
> *It seemed he'd pull a muscle each year,*
> *Which required him to just sit on his rear,*
> *But now with longer warm-ups he's been in the clear.*

I guess it'd be worth it to be able to place my poetic career on hold.

Part VIII

. . . .

Aging Gracefully

If I'd Known It Could Be So Much Fun, I'd Have Done It Sooner

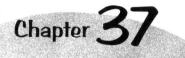

Chapter 37

· · · · · · · · · · · · · · · · ·

Lifetime Taper for a Masterful Peak

It's coming on the horizon, and I can barely contain my excitement. Yes, indeed. The event is nearing, which I now realize I've unknowingly planned my whole life around.

Just what is this monumental event? No, it's not our household finally getting caller ID. That takes a back seat. In the front seat is the fact that, in a very short time, I become a Masters Runner. I'm compiling my geriatric game plan. Getting older never felt so good. I am so psyched, I only wish I could have done it sooner.

I know this birthday will not even allow me a discount pass at the movies, so you may wonder, *what is the great significance?* Especially when I haven't really staked my name within the running hall of fame for the first 40 years of my life.

Well, after reading the latest article on peaking for a marathon, and how that process involves tapering over a three-week period, I concluded that I've been pretty much tapering for the last five years. I'm now ready to peak.

I figure if I need a little less than a month to taper for a marathon, then the direct correlation would be a systematic tapering of about half a decade for my new career as a Masters Runner. If it takes three weeks of fairly easy running with a few semi-speed workouts to prime oneself to race 26 miles, then the last five years of incomplete effort should have prepared me well to race as a Master for many, many years to come. Sounds about right to me. Hey, I put in plenty of miles before age 35. I did the training. I established a solid base from which to taper for a long time.

Now, some may question how I am to achieve this wealth of success, when my recent running career has been built on the consistency of performances that have left me off the victory stand. My conclusion is quite simple. Those similarly age-bracketed people who have been beating me at races lately are going to have burned out. Wasted. Trained too hard. Depleted. Tortoise-and-hare stuff here. Na, na, na, na, na!

They have not paced themselves as wisely as I have for the long run of life. Lactate threshold? Might be that I haven't even come close to finding mine. Tempo runs? Perhaps mine have been temporarily on hold for a while. I'm ready to test my VO_2max, as the last few years my VO_2 has been consistently at a minimum.

My slight intermission from arduous interval work will enable me to dust off and bring forth that strong Haile Gabreselaisse finishing kick at the end of the race. I have kept the delicate balance of doing just enough speed work to avoid complete atrophy and maintained the potential ability to accelerate at a higher level of fleetness. I hope.

I'm primed. My possibilities are limitless. Recent years of consistent underachieving have placed me in this lofty position. Jimmy Buffet sang "Pirate at 40." I'm singing "Peaking at 40."

Of course, I recognize there are those who might feel that, since the feeling of gazelle-like speed has not been at the forefront of my limbs for quite some time, it is irretrievable. But don't confuse *dormant* with *forever departed*. I'm certain I can reclaim it. I'm a sleeping tiger ready to pounce. Well, all right, perhaps more a caterpillar ready to shed its cocoon of sluggishness and become unfurled as a swift-floating butterfly.

I know a rendezvous with quickness is possible, because there have been those few-and-far-between days (among months of semi-slow runs) when I fortuitously experienced rapid leg turnover. I can actually momentarily relive those youthful days of speed flowing through my legs as I glide along effortlessly and take advantage of the miraculous alignment of my biorhythms. I recognize it would often take me 136 hours to recover from these infrequent encounters with speed, but sufficient training will reduce that number significantly. I think.

I know it's going to take a lot of work, and the concept of assiduous training, as opposed to just running, will have to be at the forefront of my vocabulary. But I'm ready. I've been saving myself through years of inconsistent effort. They say that rest is important for Masters Runners, and I've had more than my fair share of placidity for some time now. I'm well stocked with a solid span of repose. I have not dived into my talent pool for a while, and I'm ready to plunge into the deep waters of untapped potential.

Now, I do recognize that my theory would mean that perhaps the one who's actually done no physical activity over his or her lifetime would be in the best position to mount an assault on the Masters records. I think it's more to the benefit of the one whose body has been treading that middle-ground line between exertion and inertia. Between disuse and utilization.

Don't try and dissuade me by telling me that the strong pre-Masters Runners are continuing their dominance in the after-40 years. If that be the case, I can wait them out. I can put off the more demanding training for a few more years. Just don't forget to tell me when they begin to slow down. I can do patient peaking. I think it's worked so far.

They'll come back to me at some point. I may at least have something more to look forward to on my 80th birthday. Maybe I don't have to begin those twice-a-day training runs just yet.

Postscript: Maybe I was a little tongue in cheek with the above (or more aptly, big toe in side of shoe toebox). I've now hit 40 and with the advantage of being the new old kid on the block, I've been able to do all right in race standings. Maybe I should now begin tapering until the big 45 rolls around.

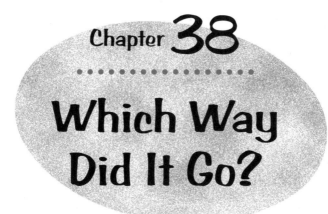

Chapter 38

Which Way Did It Go?

Every time my race results are not exactly as fast as I would have liked, and a trip down the 10K of nostalgia shows that faster days are in my rearview mirror, I often start to hum a particular song.

The song that permeates my airwaves is that old soulful one called "Love Don't Live Here Anymore." Only with me and my mental state at that juncture, the jukebox of my mind is going with the title "Speed Don't Live Here Anymore." This is what follows:

You abandoned me
Speed don't live here anymore
Just a vacancy
Speed don't live here anymore

When you lived inside my feet
There was no workout I could conceive
That you wouldn't run with me
Fatigue seemed so far away
You changed everything right away, baby

Speed don't live here anymore
Just memories of faster times
Of what I ran before
You up and went away
Found some younger legs to play, other shoes to stay

In the shuffling of my feet
Everyone can see the leisurely speed inside of me
Why'd you have to run away
Don't you know I miss you so and need your pace

Over my many years of running, I've become smarter and more experienced. However, the price I've eventually paid for wisdom is a bit of diminishing leg speed that comes with age. The only way my PRs presently seem to improve is when I suffer from the malady of memory peculiar to the more aged recollecting runner. This is otherwise known as the principle of *The older I become, the better I was.*

I admit that, on a few occasions, I shave off a few seconds when someone asks my best time for a particular distance. Okay, a few minutes. Okay, sometimes a good chunk of change. I admit to a little falsehood on my resume of running achievements at times—of my times. It's usually when I've been forced to listen to the accomplishments of some young Johnny-run-lately, and insecurity overcomes me. I do, however, stop short of referencing a fourth-place finish in the 1988 United States Olympic Marathon trials. I know the limits of the application of my fabrication.

Rest assured that my declining speed hasn't been achieved because of lack of training. It's simply a fact that my most rapid leg turnover kind of left my body somewhere between Nehru jackets and Pokemon cards. It wasn't a particular moment in time, but a steady and inevitable progression that was just a matter of time.

Now and then I am able to take a trip down that straightaway of memory lane and briefly relive those feelings of ample speed flowing through my legs. This only occurs on such prodigious occasions as when the large German shepherd down the street hops his fence and renews his desire to be my running partner by attempting to grasp onto my left thigh. A nice and natural adrenaline rush induced by my canine cohort to quickly get the heart rate up and all limbs churning with doggie dispatch.

Speed does still maintain a part-time residence within my body, although at times it feels like it's moved without leaving a forwarding address. It's now much more of a comparative concept. I may not be able to compete with my times when I was much younger, but I can muster a certain semblance of swiftness in determining how fast I can run at my age of today. This is where I'm so very thankful for what running provides and the real world doesn't. Namely, age divisions.

"It's simply a fact that my most rapid leg turnover kind of left my body somewhere between Nehru jackets and Pokemon cards."

One sign that runners are getting older is not necessarily when they realize it takes two days of warm-up to be able to achieve a full out sprint, or that the recovery period from a hard workout is only slightly less time than the Broadway run of *Cats*. The true sign of aging runners is when they begin to first examine their place in the pertinent age bracket race standings as opposed to initially looking to see where they'd finished overall.

At some point I subconsciously jumped from the competitive rationalization that others may be better because they're older, stronger, and more experienced to—they beat me because they're younger, stronger, and fresher. It's that fine line in the track of life that we all must ultimately cross.

I was no longer the neophyte looking up at the veterans, but the more ancient looking down at the youthful lightning rods.

At times it's not a pretty picture. But age-division standings sure do help our fall from pace.

There are also Clydesdale races now, with weight categories, as things get even more divided up. I haven't yet seen the award category for the best 40- to 45-year-old male humor writer in the six-foot-and-under welterweight division, but perhaps it's coming. Hey, I'd always have the option of going up or down in weight from race to race, depending on the level of competition of the runners I was going to encounter. Whatever it takes.

There are, of course, other ways to confirm the fact that one is becoming an older runner. These include the following:

1. Arrow in the foot principle. The time it takes one's Achilles tendon to loosen up in the morning is directly proportional to the number of total miles one has run in a lifetime without sufficient prerun or postrun stretching.

2. A nice 4.37K race. If you want to truly set a PR, it's no longer about searching for a downhill, point-to-point race course and praying for a tailwind at all times. And it's not about a malfunctioning race clock or an inaccurately measured course. Instead, the key now involves a little more research, and may require some travel, but guarantees a best-time performance. The solution is finding those more unique race distances that you've never raced before. You'll discover the lovely world of such things as 3K and 7.6-mile courses.

Run the race distance one time, set a new PR, and then never, ever, ever line up at that starting line again. I repeat—never. No chance of disappointment in the future with the realization your race time was slower than the year before. If you run out of distances, it means you've hung around long enough to become a race director, and you can then go ahead and feel free to create your own race length.

3. Now or then? When meeting someone new and beginning to discuss total weekly mileage, you'll realize that you are, shall I say, a more seasoned runner if you begin your reply in a certain fashion. The tell-tale sign of a more marinated runner begins with the retrospective reply. This starts with, "Well, back when I was younger I was putting in . . . ." Enough said.

4. I'm coming, I'm coming! Eventually your morning routine goes from getting up and into your run in a time equivalent to your PR for the mile to now feeling a sense of accomplishment in getting out the door within the time it takes you to complete a marathon.

5. Grecian Formula. You used to be able to tell your age-group competitors because they looked young, set themselves up near the starting line, and did a series of intimidating breakneck-speed, 50-yard sprints as a prerace warm-up. For men, the better identifying factor of those presently in your age bracket is the graying color of your competitor's hair, or that they're wearing a hat to prevent sunburn to their bald spot.

6. This ain't no warm-up. You finally must admit to yourself that your cool-down speed of many years ago is your tempo run of today.

7. No watchie, no timie. You leave your watch at home for a run on one of your old favorite courses, not because you've finally shed the addiction to knowing the exact length of time you ran. Rather, it's now because you'd simply prefer not looking at how the hands of Father Time have taken over the minute hand of your running watch.

8. Merchant of memory. Recalling some of your more successful training periods in the past, you make a renewed commitment to replicate those ways in the effort to regain that type of speed and conditioning. Five minutes into the attempt to reproduce an old track workout, you recognize that your mind has made a contract that your body can't keep. Time to renegotiate.

The truth is that it's a joy to get older as a runner. Five-year birthday increments are looked upon with great enthusiasm, as you suddenly become the youthful new kid on the block in the next age division.

And you truly can, at times, still feel swiftness in your legs, the wind whipping across your face and the ground rapidly flying by under your feet, even as you age.

Of course, you just may have to work a little harder at remembering that feeling during the seemingly prolonged intermissions between those unpredictable outbreaks of speed. Woooosh.

Part IX

. . . .

Competition and Effort

I'd Whoop My Grandma in Tiddlywinks!

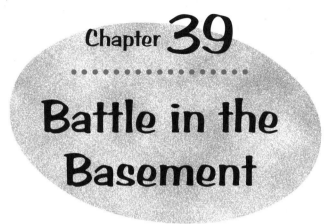

Chapter **39**

Battle in the Basement

I t's often said that pride goeth before a fall. With me, it's more like pride goeth before the wall.

I don't mean the proverbial challenger of intestinal fortitude otherwise known as the 20-mile mark of a marathon. No, I mean the wall of my basement that resides behind my treadmill.

On those cold winter running days when I decline a rendez-vous with the lovely feeling of frozen lips and jaws, I resort to the treadmill. Unfortunately, I still have the mindset of a young runner with the declining speed and energy of an aging one. Not a great combination when you also throw in those twin qualities of groundless ego and stubborn pride.

My seasonal difficulty is that I keep the speed settings on the exact same pace I used when I began some indoor running five years ago. Every succeeding winter I find it slightly more difficult to maintain that speed.

But I battle forward with the mindset of a maniacal runner, and constantly hear Winston Churchill saying, "Never, never, never give up." I doubt he had a treadmill in mind, as each time I use it I come upstairs and, through gasping breaths, say to my wife, "That thing kicked my butt." Oxygen depletion then causes me to hear a little chortle coming from a piece of exercise equipment in the basement.

But, like most runners, my dedication is as strong as my proficient ability at rationalization. I consider myself quite the expert in the explanation of SRP, otherwise known as *slower run performance*. Outdoors, I have a plethora of excuses, including the gusting wind, car traffic slowing me down, or a hilly course with too many turns.

Indoors poses a slightly different challenge, with its constant climate and the inherent difficulty of claiming you were boxed in on the treadmill. When the treadmill running first became more difficult, I began with a scientific excuse. I determined that there had been an increase in the current coming from my electrical outlet, causing greater voltage to the treadmill and a higher rate of speed—though the actual programmed pace remained the same. Yeah, yeah, that's it! I sounded like Jon Lovitz as the pathological liar from the old *Saturday Night Live* sketch.

Next year I went with a geological theme, and claimed that there must have been a shift in the earth's crust beneath my home, creating a higher grade of incline under the treadmill. A year later I concluded that since we added a room onto our house, I'd somehow diminished the quantity of available oxygen. Kind of a sea-level, high-altitude method of training.

Finally, last year, I came up with the fact that since my children were now playing in the basement more, there was, in turn, more carbon dioxide being exhaled, making running more difficult. The old invisible-vapor justification.

I'm not enough of a dunderhead to think that I will, for all eternity, be able to maintain the same speed on the treadmill or keep coming up with some half-cocked explanation each year for why the degree of difficulty seems to be increasing. I know if certain accommodations aren't ultimately made, the treadmill pace will overcome me and I'll fly off the back end of my revolving belt into my basement wall. I can envision slowly extricating my body from a six-foot hole in the wall, kicking the plaster chunks from my running shoes, and shaking the paint particles off the back of my head.

As I then explain the situation to my wife (who by then will have responded to the sonic boom sound from the basement), she'll undoubtedly ask, "Well then, why didn't you just slow the pace down a little?"

Ah yes, I'll think to myself. I will have just pulled myself out from being lodged within my basement wall, and she'll offer logic! We're not talking logic here; we're talking running!

You want sound reasoning from someone who mixes chocolate energy gel in their milk for breakfast and who pins and re-pins his race number an average of 23 times to get it feeling just right on his shirt. You're looking for common sense from one who, when completely drenched from running in a torrential downpour, moves off the sidewalk to avoid getting wet from an approaching lawn sprinkler. You want logic from one who convinces himself a running injury doesn't really exist if an ample dosage of pain relievers allows him to limp through a short run without crying. Logic escapes me faster than the sprint for cinnamon rolls at the postrace refreshment table.

My less-than-pragmatic runner thought process dictated that I come up with a solution other than simply slowing the speed down. The conclusion I arrived at may seem a little expensive, but there's no price for a runner's peace of mind.

It was time to get a new treadmill. Recognizing the slight variance between treadmills and their actual versus stated speeds, I decided it was time to begin again with a new speed setting on a new treadmill.

This time I'm going to pick a pace that I should also be able to handle in five years. I'd hate to have to truly replace that basement wall.

Chapter 40

Nocturnal Decathlon

My wife was not really involved in team sports as a child. Her desire for athletic competition was pretty much in a perpetually nonexistent state. I recall, years ago, playing with her in a coed, 3-on-3 basketball tournament where the game was going on a little longer than she'd anticipated. At that point she turned to me and said, through deep breaths of indifference, "Can't we just let them win?"

She achieved her goal of game completion rather quickly, as I was so flabbergasted by her question that she threw me entirely off my game. From that point on we went down to defeat rather briskly. I sulked away and it took me two days to get over defeat, while she forgot about losing within three seconds of the winning basket.

This was a clue that she was apparently not raised with the *eye-gouge to victory* philosophy, or the athletic-competition mentality of *winning isn't everything, it's the only thing*. On the other hand, I had the competitive nature of wanting to kick my grandmother's butt at gin rummy. I know you don't get a lot of bragging rights around the water cooler with that triumph. But I didn't care, and often had to restrain myself from doing a victory dance around her family room while waving my cards in the air.

I was also the type to wake up every morning and read an inspirational quote that has been framed next to many a runner's bedside:

> **E**very morning in Africa, a gazelle wakes up. It knows it must outrun the fastest lion or it will be killed. Every morning in Africa, a lion wakes up. It knows it must run faster than even the slowest gazelle, or it will starve. It doesn't matter whether you're a lion or gazelle—when the sun comes up, you'd better be running.

When my wife first read this quote upon arising, she simply stated, "I live in the Midwest. Last I looked, there ain't no lions or gazelles here. I'm going downstairs to have a bowl of Cap'n Crunch while you go ahead and figure out which African animal you are."

It was quite apparent she didn't buy into the competitive runner's psyche. Nonetheless, over time, my penchant for running finally got to her, and she started to do a little light jogging for exercise. While her feet were just testing the waters, I'd jumped full body overboard in concluding she'd soon be challenging herself in 5Ks, performing intervals with me at the track, doing tempo runs around our neighborhood, and beginning training for her first marathon.

Guess again, old zealous one. I failed to realize that tapping dormant stores of competitive athletic juices might require a wee bit of excavating. My wife seemed to train by the motto of the venerable runner, Walter Stack, who said his method of training was to "start slowly and then taper off." She peaked before she began.

But then something quite surprising happened. With the birth of our first child, my wife's competitive drive, as well as her athletic talents, began to emerge. It was the old walkie-talkie baby monitor contraption that first exposed my wife's true cutthroat nature.

She is indeed athletically competitive; she just needed the right event. Our baby provided that, as each night we engaged in the event of the nocturnal decathlon. It was an event that required the winner to respond to the waking call of the baby the fastest by getting to his room before the other.

Now I know some may think, why get involved? Why not just roll over at 2:00 A.M. and let her fully assume this parental obligation that she so desired? Well, being the shameless competitor that I am, I couldn't sleep idly by while my wife tried to set a new speed record from our room to the baby's room each night. I didn't want her coming back to bed and gleefully telling me about her new PR. There was a race going on right in my house each night and no entry fees were required. No race T-shirt was provided, but at least I didn't have to travel far to the starting line.

This was all about the lion and gazelle. All right, it was an absurd matter of a runner's competitive drive run amok. But hey, I figured I could at least get in some cross-training.

Each night we found ourselves answering the bell for this race. I knew my wife's compulsion to win had heated up when I came home early one afternoon and found her practicing her hurdle technique over our couch in the family room.

The play by play for our competition went something like this:

"Welcome to the nocturnal decathlon, where I will serve as your announcer and color commentator.

"If our cameraman can pull back, we can take a look at tonight's course. It will bring us from their bed, over the large bedroom loveseat, around the dresser and exercise machine, down one flight of 16 stairs, around the corner to the left, and through a set of swinging doors. Finally, over the family room furniture, down the 30-foot straightaway toward their son's room, a quick left into the room, and a dodge around the changing table to his crib. An event of speed, stamina, and grace.

"We are ready to begin, as all three participants are sound asleep. Just as I speak, sounds are coming from the monitor! We have a

clean start, and both parents have gone from a slumbering state to a full sprint in 0.8 seconds! Great reaction time!

"Being in the inside lane, Mrs. Schwartz is able to grab an early lead. The first obstacle is the large bedroom loveseat. Mr. Schwartz opts for the diving method by leaping directly over the couch and belly smacking on the floor. Mrs. Schwartz's flexibility and strength suit her here, as she uses the loveseat as a pommel horse, placing both hands on the back and flipping over and onto her feet. Now is when their power training comes into play.

"Approaching the staircase, our competitors are neck and neck, as Mrs. Schwartz uses the two-arm swivel maneuver on the banister, which allows her to swing around into position to attack the downhill course. Mr. Schwartz is forced to take the outside lane, losing valuable time.

"The disparity in leg length comes into play, as the latter is now bounding and juking down the stairs with an impressive three-step stride. His off-season work on the Stairmaster seems to have helped. Mrs. Schwartz has elected to go with the sprinter's style, concentrating on her speed and attacking each step separately.

"They both push off the last step at almost the same time, and we can see their look of determination as they plow through the swinging doors, jump over the family room ottoman, and dash down the hallway. We're going to have an exciting finish, as they jostle for position.

"Mrs. Schwartz, on the inside left lane, will have the distinct advantage of making a short quick turn directly into the baby's room. As we now see, that will indeed be the margin of victory in tonight's nocturnal decathlon, as she is able to grab the lead at the end in a near photo finish!

"It is warm to see how our competitors now share a bottle of water, a towel, and a warm embrace. Sportsmanship is important, and Mr. Schwartz indicates he won't contest the finish results with a request for an instant-replay review.

"Please join us tomorrow night for another exciting presentation of nocturnal decathlon."

It was quite interesting to see the development of the competi-tive, athletic side of my wife. She did keep things in perspective, while I, on the other hand, was lost in the rivalry, keeping close track of my win-loss record and my split times at various stages of the event, while devising training methods to improve my speed. I set up a video camera in the family room to analyze my style over the last leg of the event. Perspective for me was pretty much lost. If I ever really even possessed it.

Our baby did finally grasp the concept of sleeping through the night, and no longer served as the starting pistol for our late-night athletic contest. Not wanting to entirely give up on any home athletic competition, we were only left with the duel of the short sprint to the front door when we heard the mail plop through the chute. Just wasn't the same.

I'm thinking of challenging her to 43 times around the garage after I install the steeplechase hurdle and water jump in the back-yard. That might work.

Chapter 41

Yo, Einstein! Recognize a Pattern Here?

We runners are often bombarded by motivational words seeking to make the meek into the mighty. Or at least the snail into the gazelle.

From *Just do it,* to *When the going gets tough, the tough go running,* we're sold on the premise that effort breeds results. I've got a slightly modified take. I say, effort is key, but look a little to your breeder to predict your results.

Don't get me wrong. I still latch onto all those inspirational credos. I'm a sucker for a motivating quote. I confess to having running T-shirts with sayings like, *If you can believe it, the mind will achieve it.* But without trying to cause Norman Vincent Peale to roll over in his grave—the train of positive thinking may get derailed before you reach your intended destination.

Now, just hear me out before you start labeling me as a running heretic and try to tar and feather me with analgesic ointment.

Here are the facts. My vertical leap hasn't improved since kindergarten, as I wasn't born with the nickname "Springs." No matter how much I may have positive thoughts of tomahawk dunks dancing in my head, the only way I'm going to jam a basketball is with a powerful trampoline. On an eight-foot basket.

Similarly, given that my running PRs may have seen better days, the reality is I can use positive thinking until my biofeedback is stuffed, but the only way I'm ever going to see 2:35 on the marathon-finish-line clock is as a spectator.

Hold tight. You don't need to start opening your motivational toolbox or inviting me to jump on the bandwagon of encouragement. I still believe it's better to have tried and failed than never to have tried at all. And I often hear the words of Thomas Edison saying, "Genius is 1 percent inspiration and 99 percent perspiration," and even of Walt Disney himself, saying, "If you can dream it, you can do it." My internal playback of motivational quotes is well stocked.

My pragmatic philosophy is, inspiration is good. However, perspiration will take you only so far—if you want to be a speed demon with the acceleration abilities of the Mach 1, you'd best be selective in choosing your parents. The gene pool my legs were wading in wasn't exactly full of the fastest currents in the water. Ma and Pa weren't to be confused with the speed creatures Marion Jones and Maurice Greene. More like Tommie Turtle and Sally Snail.

My light bulb began going off when I was 14 years old and hell-bent on being a great 100-meter sprinter. Problem was my all out sprint was fairly equivalent to the speed of others as they jogged during their post-workout cool-down.

At the beginning of a race it appeared that I was going in the wrong direction, since everyone was pulling away from me so quickly. Kind of an optical illusion, while I was operating under a speed delusion. As if I had any.

By the time I approached the finish line, I usually had to jump an obstacle or two as the next event, the 110-meter high hurdles, was already being set up. Other runners were left wondering which race I'd been participating in.

To this day, I still hear the rhetorical question of my junior high school track coach after I'd finished last in the 100-meter dash for the 42nd consecutive race. He said, "Kid, do you seem to notice a pattern here?"

That was only slightly less painful to hear than my teammate saying, "Yo, numbskull. Wake up and smell the Gatorade." It was finally dawning on me that if all my competitors simultaneously fell down halfway through the race, they'd still have time to get up, dust themselves off, tighten their shoelaces, get a drink, wave to their mothers in the stands, and then proceed to nip me at the finish.

At the time I started to realize that the label *world's fastest human* would not be uttered in the same breath as my name, I also uncovered the wisdom of an eighth-grade anatomy teacher. I took some solace in learning a little about muscle fibers being either fast twitch or slow twitch. Up until then the only thing middle school science had done for me was give me a nervous twitch.

I'd enthusiastically discovered that my languid legs could be chalked up to an insufficient amount of fast twitch fibers. On the bright side, I was well stocked in the slow twitch variety, which meant endurance was my forte. The only way I was going to win a sprint was if I could somehow convince the other participants that we need to race say, maybe, 89 consecutive times with a 30-second rest in between. Slow would eventually prevail over fast. Twitch, that is. However, I highly doubted I'd be able to convince the sprinters to continue racing with my words of, "Hey, Rocket Boy. Line 'em up again. That's only 87. We're almost there. I'm gaining on you, Johnny Jetpack!"

I left behind the world of missile-velocity sprinters and starting blocks, as I determined that the more times the race required one to circle the track, the better I did. I'd have made a good gerbil.

Although I still have a T-shirt that reads, *Sweat plus sacrifice equals success*, I know the reality of it all. I'm thinking of coming out with my own shirt. It'll say, *With no twitches of fast, in the sprints you'll be last. But if your twitches are slow, oh, the distance you can go!*

Chapter 42

Best Laid Plans

Ever have those days where your shoelaces come untied in the first mile, the wind seems to be hounding you no matter which direction you turn, and last night's spicy Italian dinner is doing repeat intervals in your esophagus?

Those times where the Band-Aid on your toe has chosen to migrate down your sock and provide you a lovely blister, while you begin to feel an allergic reaction to your new shirt, the drawcord on your running shorts just snapped, and your Walkman batteries died a quarter of the way into a long run? Those moments where you must use your sleeve to wipe off your cheek as you reflect upon the veracity of Jim Croce's lyrical advice to not spit into the wind? Those vexing occasions where you wondered, for just a split second, whether those couch potatoes were actually on to something?

At those times I think of Edward Murphy. Not Eddie the comedian and actor, and not a new, speedy, indoor 1500-meter runner from Ireland. No, this is the Edward whose words contributed greatly to our nomenclature. Words usually muttered by someone with a look of profound disbelief, head shaking from side to side.

As the story goes, Mr. Murphy was one of the engineers on some rocket-sled experiments performed by the United States Air Force in 1949. The goal was to test the tolerance of humans to the forces of acceleration. You know those pictures where the force of the air makes the guy's face look like it's being pressed as hard as possible against a sheet of glass and his lips are pushed up somewhere above his eyebrows? That's the force of acceleration. I think the fact that I never could put together a real fast 400-meter time is because my body just can't stand the forces of acceleration very well. I'd probably undergo spontaneous combustion at too fast a pace.

One of the experiments involved a set of 16 accelerometers (sounds like something one could use, say, somewhere around marathon mile 23) mounted to different parts of the hesitant volunteer's body. There were two ways each sensor could be glued, and, in a Herculean feat of ineptitude, somebody quite ably managed to install all 16 the wrong way around!

> **"If there are two or more ways to do something, and one of those ways can result in a catastrophe, then someone will do it."**
>
> **–Edward Murphy**

Now comes Mr. Murphy's contribution to history. Immediately after this installation debacle, Edward made his pronouncement to a group of reporters. The popularity of his words spread throughout the land and achieved that prodigious honor of being included in the 1958 Webster's Dictionary.

You ask, what were old Edward's wonderful words of wisdom? Never to be known as the oracle of optimism, Mr. Murphy was more the pundit of pessimism in providing his perspective on life. He said, "If there are two or more ways to do something, and one of those ways can result in a catastrophe, then someone will do it."

Hence, Murphy's Law. Its more modern version being, *Whatever can go wrong, will go wrong*, or *I knew I should have just laid silently in bed all day today.*

The fact is that, at times, his words do ring true within the realm of running. Certainly there are those occasions when your personal blueprints don't line right up with that thing existing beyond the borders of the planning stage—something called *reality*.

Those times when you diligently train for months for a particular race. Then, when the big day arrives, your car battery has died, you eventually get to the race and discover your preregistration form was never received, you forgot to put your running shorts on under your sweats, your bladder feels like it's about to burst as there was a mix-up with the arrival of the port-a-johns, and the weather brings a torrential downpour and howling winds. Dealing with all these obstacles, you begin the race, and by mile 3 it already feels as though Mr. Murphy has jumped aboard for a piggyback ride.

The principle of Murphy's Law, as applied to running, includes the following (and given that Mr. Murphy was probably more into skydiving than running, these are more aptly titled—Schwartz's Laws):

Schwartz's Law of Traffic Signals

When you're cruising along with the euphoria of endorphins in full bloom, with no hint of fatigue and in no need or desire of a rest, the traffic signals will always be red at the intersection—requiring you to stop your effortless pace. When your legs feel like massive lead trunks chained to steel wrecking balls, and you could use an unscheduled 30-second rest break—the traffic signals will inevitably always be green.

Schwartz's Law of Achievement

You set a personal-record race time on a new 10K course, and feel convinced that your hard-core training is finally paying off. When you proceed to share your accomplishment by bragging to anyone within a 40-mile radius about your achievement, it will be published a week later in the local paper that the course was actually 300 yards short.

Schwartz's Law of Conversation

As you ride the shuttle bus to the race starting line, you'll be pumping yourself up, getting into your game-face mode, and obtaining the proper psychological mindset. You'll then find yourself seated next to a first-time racer and incessant talker, who needs to share with you in agonizing detail every single entry from their training log of the last eight months, as well as their history of ingrown toenails. As you learn about his prerace diet and gastrointestinal tendencies, you then discover he plans to run exactly the same pace as you. He'll then propose to be your new loquacious running partner over the next 26.2 miles and keep you going with his enthusiastic chatter, while you begin looking for an extra sock to shove in his mouth.

Schwartz's Law of Timepieces

You've pushed yourself near the limits and completed a race-simulated run that you believe has topped last year's time for the same course. You'll then check your fancy, brand new, aerodynamically shaped running watch with 100-hour chronograph, recessed graphics, polyurethane strap, and 10-hour countdown timer, and haplessly see that it's not working.

Schwartz's Law of Being Seen By the Herd

Runners are usually content to bask in the glow of their personal achievement and don't need accolades from others. But darn tootin' if we don't appreciate being noticed cruising the neighborhood when we're running like poetry in motion. Problem is you'll be seen by more people than invitees to a Puff Daddy birthday party when you're running with the speed of cold molasses flowing uphill and the only poetry you resemble is a rhymeless and incoherent limerick.

Of course, on the days when you're gracefully running rapidly along the pavement there won't be a soul to be seen within ten square miles. It's then that you consider knocking on neighbors' doors, wondering if they'd have any interest in sitting on their front lawn to admire you while you smoothly stride up and down the street.

Schwartz's Law of Enlightenment

When the repairman comes to fix the belt on your treadmill, he will calibrate the speed and advise you that the numbers are off. You would need to add 20 seconds to the timed pace per mile that is flashing on the screen to be accurate. Any of those indoor tempo run training miles you've put in over the last two years have actually been much slower than you'd proudly given yourself credit for.

Despite the applicability, at times, of Murphy's Law to running, I doubt old Edward was a runner. If he were, then instead of holding a press conference and announcing his principles of pessimism after his acceleration test fiasco, he would have simply gone for a nice, easy five-mile jaunt to relieve the stress.

Then, just maybe, we'd instead be talking about Edward's Law. Of ebullience.

Chapter 43

Running Matters

I never wanted to be a pushy parent and put running shoes on my kids before they could walk, or have their first sentence be, "What's my split time?" I thought they'd probably become runners by osmosis, or at least by having been drizzled with enough of my running sweat over the years.

Chalk another one up to myopia. I soon realized that they were going to have their own interests and pursuits, and those just might not include repeat quarter-miles with a half-lap jog in between.

I first began to question my prior wisdom when one year I corralled my older son to watch the famous Boston Marathon on TV with me. Seeing the race unfold, I envisioned how he was probably thinking about challenging himself, contemplating testing the limits of his own stamina. So I casually asked him whether he thought he'd want to participate in a marathon someday. A bit too quickly, he responded, "Are you kidding? No way. Uh-uh. Nothing doing. I ain't getting that tired. Ever. I've seen some of those guys at the finish line. I'll stick with my motorized scooter, thank you very much!"

218 I Run, Therefore I Am—Nuts!

I stared back with profound disbelief, as my bubble was burst like a half-filled paper cup of water being flung to the pavement. What about that old, apple-doesn't-fall-far-from-the-tree thing? Wasn't that supposed to apply here? I was realizing that perhaps the running shoes had fallen far, far away from the starting line. Heck, at this rate, it didn't look like those shoes were even going to touch his feet.

It then dawned on me that my children might not have been born with thoughts of interval workouts dancing in their head. Nonetheless, I couldn't help but long to hear those magical and phenomenal words, "Hey Dad, how about we put in a couple of miles before dinner?"

That would get my heart rate up but, for many years, the closest I'd gotten was "Hey Dad, on your run, do you mind going by the video store and picking up a movie?" When I would give in to that request, I'd often edit the potential selections and bring home running-related films such as *Chariots of Fire, Running Brave, Without Limits, Personal Best,* and *Endurance.* Subtlety wasn't necessarily my strong suit when it came to running.

> "I'm the same guy who tried to explain to my infant children the finer points of pacing after we'd read *The Tortoise and the Hare,* and told them all about the Boston Marathon's Heartbreak Hill as I read *The Little Engine That Could.*"

I'm the same guy who tried to explain to my infant children the finer points of pacing after we'd read *The Tortoise and the Hare,* and told them all about the Boston Marathon's Heartbreak Hill as I read *The Little Engine That Could.* Their pajamas were T-shirts from my races, and their first exposure to a sandbox was the long-jump pit at the local high school track. I taught them how to add by discussing split times, and they learned the metric system from track and field events. Their versions of lullabies were "Ain't No Stoppin' Us Now" by McFadden and Whitehead, or "Born to Run" by Bruce Springsteen. Okay, so maybe I was a little bit pushy.

Lo and behold, one day, out of nowhere, my younger son inquired whether he could go for a run with me. Before you could say Arthur Lydiard, I had my running shoes on, a short course charted out, water bottles chilling for our return, and I'd handed the video camera off to my wife. I was enthusiastically standing by the back door, like an out-of-control dog frantically wagging its tail and wildly jumping up and down after being asked if it wanted to go for a walk. Adrenaline out of control!

As we ventured out, I felt like a nervous teenager on a first date; I wanted everything to go off without a hitch. Or at least without a side stitch. Not too fast, avoid the hills, go with the wind at our backs, tell jokes, not too far, keep the conversation flowing.

As we began, I thought about how he was gaining an appreciation for the importance of health, an understanding of discipline and commitment, the drive to improve. In actuality, he was thinking, *Won't my friends think I'm cool if they see me? Maybe Dad will get me a neat sweat suit that I can wear to school. I wonder if I can steer him in the direction of the ice cream store. If I run a race, do they have T-shirts in my size?*

Over the years we continued to run on and off, and, at times, I gained an even greater appreciation for commitment—the parental kind. Like the time I overextended myself on a workout in the morning and spent the rest of the day playing the musical furniture game, gravitating from couch to chair to bed. Then, of all days, and just before I was dozing off for a nap, my son says, "Hey Dad, let's go for a run."

In leaning toward opting for a rain check, I tried to add to his expanding vocabulary with an explanation of muscle fiber breakdown, Achilles tendonitis, and pounding joints.

He replied, "Yeah, yeah, whatever. C'mon. Lace 'em up, big fella. Which direction do you want to go?"

Talk about the old internal conflict. Part of me remained glued to the couch, while part of me thought, *Get out there with him. Show him something about mental fortitude, reservoirs of strength, and the will of a champion. Get your butt off the canvas and fight on, buddy!*

Mr. Emotion was persuasive, and before I knew it, we were out the door and moving down the sidewalk. Don't tell me about glycogen reserves. That was all about parental reserves. I also rationalized it might be good training for simulating the last mile of a marathon.

In my delirium, I thought of the line *Whatever doesn't destroy me, makes me strong*. I concluded that if I made it back home in one piece I'd pretty much consider myself invincible.

We did make it back without my nine-year-old having to roll me home after his dad passed out from exhaustion in the neighbor's front yard shrubbery. I am running parent, hear me roar!

Over the years, as with a lot of things at their ages, running flows in and out of my children's lives. But I'm cautiously optimistic that someday we'll toe it up at a race and really go head to head. Dad-o a son-o!

And with a little prerace banter, I could utter those wonderful words, "Lace 'em up tight, little guy! You're going to eat my dust!"

But I know parental pride would prevail, and that would be one time I wouldn't mind too much if somebody kicked my butt. I think.

Part X

. . . .

Motivation

To Thine Own Sole Be True

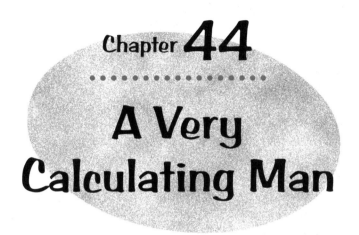

Chapter 44

A Very Calculating Man

I'm a great believer that each of us possesses a particular area of expertise. Some a little more eccentric than others, but a talent nonetheless.

I always wished my greatest aptitude would be something admirable, like superb running ability and an Olympic-marathon-trials qualifying time. Instead, I was resigned to the fact that perhaps my talents were a little less enviable and more in line with how many grapes I could stuff in my mouth without choking, or a lifetime of successive races run without being able to achieve a negative split.

Nonetheless, I continued to be on the lookout for some type of talent that truly set me above the crowd. I'm now here to proudly state that after years of fruitless searching, I've finally arrived at my particular, albeit peculiar, area of expertise. Just call me the Matrix Man of Running Performance. Computation king.

I can tell you, off the top of my head, exactly how long it will take you to run a specific distance at a certain pace. I'm a walking, talking, running computer. I could barely master algebra in ninth grade, but after years of continuous studying of pace charts and various running-related calculators (reflecting one's time at various distances and at various paces), I've developed the skill to be a virtual time determiner of many different types of running results. Some may select a hobby of studying to learn a foreign language or concentrate on increasing the value of their stock portfolio. I had much more important information to focus on. I studied interval pace calculators and finish time predictor charts.

I, like many racing runners, became immersed in numbers of time, speed, length, splits, personal records, and so on. Numbers would help us stay motivated, challenged, and inspired. We chased them, were preoccupied with them, studied them, memorized them, and became infatuated by them.

I advanced from the basic studies of determining one's time at a particular race distance if supplied with the per mile pace. That was kindergarten class. Abacus stuff. I was at a postgraduate level, getting a doctorate in race pace computation.

Determining your time for a marathon if you ran 8:23 per mile? I can spit that answer out in 0.6 seconds. Heck, I can calculate your total time if you tell me you anticipate running the first 9 miles of the flat-terrain course in 8:15 per mile; there are rolling hills which occur for the next 3 1/2 miles and you anticipate slowing down 10 seconds per mile; you plan to take a walking break for 345 yards at mile 15, and then resume your initial pace plus 8 seconds per mile for the next 6 miles; whereupon you take your customary potty break and aid station refueling, and with a resurgence of muscle activity and human spirit, you summon all energy to finish with the remaining miles at an 8:12 pace. I'll even supply your average pace including or excluding the mandatory port-a-john stop and walking break, and further calculate for you how a head wind of 14.8 miles per hour for 8 miles of the race and a 97 percent humidity level would affect your total time.

When I volunteer at races and call out the split times, I can also compute and provide your projected finish time. Sometimes that's not the most welcome or motivating bit of information to have, but Calculating Man is there for you if you need him.

I'm also quadra-modal, as I can give you your speed per mile or per kilometer, in miles per hour or kilometers per hour. I'm also working on meters per second, which is big in some European countries. I speak all known languages of pace and measurement.

I'm also the master of conversion. Throw a kilometer number at me and, within three seconds, I'll give you the equivalent miles down to the thousandths decimal place.

I'm ready for the *Tonight Show,* or at least a summer job as a carnival barker at running expos. I'm an ambulatory, talking, data processor of split times and more. An analytical engine of anticipated pace. And to think I was previously calculus-challenged.

With all my calculating abilities, I'm beginning to construct a computation model of my own. Give me your age; average number of miles per week run over last 14 weeks; number of running magazines subscribed to; whether you ran track in high school and, if so, your best 2-mile time as a 17-year-old; how long you can hold a hamstring stretch; whether you refuel within 30 minutes of a run; number of races entered in the last six months; whether you do speedwork; whether you rotate your running shoes; and your best 10K when you didn't taper beforehand. Then I'll give you your anticipated race time from the 60-meter high hurdles to a 50-mile, rugged-terrain trail race. Heck, I might even be able to accurately estimate your javelin throw within six feet or so.

But don't ask me anything about converting Celsius to Fahrenheit, or the speed of sound. I know my limitations of expertise. However, if it helps with your motivation to know how fast you should be able to run a mile based on your most recent 8K; how many calories you burned during the latter; what your present body mass index is; what pace you should be running your easy runs in; and how that time correlates to a 21-miler on a flat course, then I'm your calculating man.

Just give me a call. Though I might have to look up my phone number for you. I always have a tough time remembering those non-running-related numbers.

Chapter 45

Procrastinate Now

I read an article by some upper-echelon runners in which they indicated they never had too much difficulty getting outside and putting in their daily miles in a timely manner. They lived by a specific time schedule as to when a workout would begin and stuck to it. This only served to confirm my belief that these elite runners were obviously not swimming near the same gene pool as those like myself.

Never had any problems immediately getting going? Stick to a schedule? Heck, often times when my morning run finally begins, I've already had problems getting out of bed, finding the bathroom, staying awake while brushing my teeth, and not short-circuiting the house while making coffee.

I'd start my day debating that influential little man in my head who said, *Go for a run later. Just sit down on the couch, grab the newspaper and remote control, have a Danish, and kick off those running shoes.* Apparently those elite runners never heard the voice of this slovenly anti-accomplisher.

The problem began for me many years ago. My first college roommate was the master of procrastination. Later wasn't good enough for him. He could calmly go beyond later. His philosophy was that hard work pays out over time, but laziness pays off now. His credo was, the quicker he fell behind in his classwork, the more time he'd have to catch up. His life was a continuous filibuster. Skilled in the art of stalling.

The ensuing years enabled me to perfect the craft of procrastination, and I actually became quite accomplished. I suddenly found, at times, my planned early morning runs occurred closer to midnight. I'd always eventually get my run in, but back then I'd officially begun my quest to qualify as a true procrastinator—those who are proud of their ability to get around to it later.

My philosophy developed that the longer the run or more difficult the workout to be completed, the more insignificant and lengthy the work that needed to be done before beginning. In other words, the law of inverse excuses. I'd always thought of this as harmless inaction. If I didn't have any other commitments, then there wasn't really any problem with my loitering around the house until my running shoes finally hit pavement and off I went.

Now, there were indeed plenty of days when there would be no hesitation, and I'd be out the door with my shoes hitting the road quite timely. My feet-like-the-elite days. Other times, I'd find myself concentrating on the less meaningful distractions of perusing Web sites devoted to Venezuelan crock-pot cooking, or checking out the Norwegian Olympic track and field best results from the 1960s. Seeking sufficient motivation, I'd begin leafing through my collection of running magazines of the last two decades. Always an easy way to kill six hours or so.

My procrastinating tactics continued on fairly regularly until, years later, my older son became a member of the homework brigade. It was quite apparent that the foot-dragging apple hadn't fallen far from the loitering tree, as I'd watch him spend three hours alphabetizing 739 baseball cards before beginning a little spelling homework.

I knew he was simply emulating my art of procrastination. Not something that I could really take a lot of parental pride in. I'd been busted for my belatedness. If I procrastinated before a run I couldn't really call him on the carpet for stalling with his homework.

That's when a surge of fear rushed straight through me. I was going to have to change. I needed to kick the dilatory habit. No longer could a Sunday morning be spent listening repetitively to the theme music from *Chariots of Fire*, searching for motivation for a long run, all the while feeling more like Jackson Browne's "Running on Empty." My son had been watching me and copying me. To make matters worse, I had to change immediately. I could no longer live by the paradoxical philosophy of *procrastinate now*!

So I became slightly like the elite runners, and began to take up residence in heretofore uncharted territory—the land of timely accomplishment.

Oh, I still delay from time to time, like finally doing Tuesday's interval workout on Thursday, or finishing this essay, which I began in 1997. Hey, some said a story on procrastination couldn't ever be completed. Well, it might be many years later, but I sure showed them.

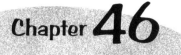

Chapter 46

Twin Theories of Running Resourcefulness

Einstein had nothing on the genius of runners. Oh, he might have had the superb intelligence to come up with his *Theory of Relativity* and the old $E=mc^2$ thingamajig. For whatever that's worth. But we runners couldn't care less about energy being equal to mass times the speed of light. We're more concerned with our lack of energy if our mass increases and produces the speed of fright.

We need more practical ideas. More useful stuff. That's why we've come up with our own theories to help keep us motivated. The first is the *Theory of Running Relativity* and the second is the *Runner's Theory of Rationalization*. Two resourceful methods to never allow the facts to get in the way of the results.

The first theory became necessary when we discovered that $A^2=ST,SOG!$ (Advancing Age equals Slower Times, Son of a Gun!). We had to come up with something to help our motivation. We then discovered that it's all relative.

Runner's ingenuity has not only given us waffle-soled shoes and simulated high altitude sleeping tents but, most importantly, the relativity of age-equivalent performance tables. These tables are designed for those of us who failed to be bursting with unbridled enthusiasm with declining racing times as we got older. This lovely theoretical model takes into account your age and present race performance, and determines a comparable time if the race were run at a specific younger age. What a concept! I can be better than I'd ever been before. Relatively speaking of course.

I may be getting slower, getting older, losing my hair and flexibility, and have a decreasing maximum heart rate, but with the running relativity theory, I'm actually the best I ever was!

This is the type of information that helps keeps one showing up at the starting line. What better motivation is there than to discover that with your current 10K time you could, with everything being relative, kick your butt of yesteryear. Heck, to psych yourself up for a race you may find yourself engaging in trash talking at your old racing photographs. That's clearly the epitome of competing against oneself.

> **"I may be getting slower, getting older, losing my hair, my flexibility and have a decreasing maximum heart rate, but with the running relativity theory, I'm actually the best I ever was!"**

Not only do runners have their theory of relativity as applied to age related information but there are also tables to help you determine, based on your present time at a particular distance, what time you should be able to finish in a race of another distance. Take your present half marathon time and determine, theoretically, what you should right now be able to run a 5K in. Life should be so predictable. Plug in the fact it previously took 43 minutes to travel the 27 miles to the airport during morning rush-hour traffic, and then be able to determine how long the trip should take if done midday, in a strong rain, with road construction eliminating two lanes of the three-lane expressway for a 4 1/2-mile stretch. That's useful information to have.

Now, here's where the theory of rationalization comes into play. I recall being a little disheartened when I discovered that I couldn't meet my theoretically equivalent marathon time, based on my 10K time. I thought that maybe I wasn't pushing myself hard enough in the marathon. Maybe I was starting out too fast. Maybe I wasn't refueling sufficiently. Maybe I wasn't tapering correctly. Well, I concluded that maybe I was just looking at all this the wrong way. Maybe the running shoe was actually half full! The power of rationalization finally made it all very clear. It had nothing to do with underachieving in the marathon. The fact was I was definitely an overachieving runner in the 10K! Hey, I might not be able to race with the leaders, but I sure can rationalize with the best of them.

Heck, poor times for me at some race distances can only serve to magnify the overachieving brilliance of my performances at other distances. The worse I did here, the better I am there! You can never fail with the runner's theory of rationalization!

Maybe I was actually achieving elsewhere much more than should reasonably be expected. The fact that I could never get a soufflé to rise might really mean that I've gone well beyond my natural culinary talents given that I can actually get breadcrumbs to stick to my eggplant parmigiana! Or perhaps my inability to master origami and successfully make one of those little paper swans really means I'm overachieving with the fact I can create a paper airplane that flys more than seven feet!

Einstein can have his old postulate about the physical laws of nature. We've got our own physical laws of running with the twin theories of resourcefulness to help us interpret the performances of today as being better than yesterday and not nearly as good as tomorrow.

We've got the ingenuity. We've got the resources. We're willing to do whatever it takes for the best of times. Literally. Hey, once you master the art of rationalizing, anything is relatively possible.

Chapter 47

The Motivator in the Hat

Confession time. What runner amongst us has not wrestled with the internal interrogation as to whether we were going to engage in a run on a particular day? It wasn't the question of perhaps running later in the day, but a question of doing it at all.

Peter Maher, a Canadian Olympian and sub 2:12 marathoner, summed it up well in providing the runner's rule of punctuation. He said, "Running is a big question mark that's there each and every day. It asks you, 'Are you going to be a wimp or are you going to be strong today?'."

I admit there are some days when the invitation to join the Kingdom of Wimps is pretty darn strong and I have to do all I can to avoid being named Prime Minister in the Land of Pansies. Didn't all runners experience those MMIA days otherwise know as *Motivation Missing in Action*? Didn't we all have those moments where it would be easier to break into Fort Knox with a toothpick than it would be to convince oneself to get out the front door?

I sure thought so until Mr. Gold Medalist Frank Shorter burst my bubble of belief that all runners experienced some difficulty, from time to time, with inspiration for raising their rate of respiration. He claimed he never had any difficulty getting out the door for his run! Well it then became clear what separated us.

He had quite different doors than I did! It wasn't different genes. It was the difference in the hardware of our hatchways.

The doors of the elite must be equipped with speakers that provide soothing motivational words, quotes from their competitors, or uplifting music. I needed to find out at which *Home Depot* they were shopping.

At times my door appeared to be saying "Yo ignoramus. Don't even think about coming through me. It ain't happening buddy. Now take those silly little colorful running shorts off and get back under those blankets. See you another day nimrod knees. What in Sam Shoelaces were you even thinking!"

Other days my door just stood in mock silence while I got dressed. I was certain I next heard a faint snicker as I proceeded to run outside into a torrential downpour.

Everyone has his or her own approach to motivation and I eventually figured out that what works best is what often comes quite naturally for me. Namely, don't even think. That's a very simple concept, which I can often accomplish with innate ease. Basically, if I don't even think of not going then it can't become an option. My even-handed and empty-headed approach to motivation. No mind, no matter.

I know from talking to other runners that there are occasions when motivation is a little light and it'd be a lot easier if Mr. Shorter was your roommate or Coach Jack Daniels was sitting in your family room providing a voice of encouragement. How perfect if we all had a little motivating person who'd keep us going with words of wit and wisdom as well as training information. Maybe someone persuasive, amusing, and knowledgeable about everything. Somebody that arrived on a day when the door seemed to have 47 bolts and padlocks stopping you from going running.

Somebody that could provide some compelling words to help out Joe and Josie on-and-off-again runners rejoin the middle-of-the-pack. Somebody, say, like the ***Motivator in the Hat***.

This is the story of such a strange yet compelling visitor as it was told to me:

I. Fortuitous Meeting?

The sun was far behind clouds
It seemed way too wet to run.
I sat glumly in the health club
Not expecting any fun.

So in that old gym
Right there I sat.
And pondered my options
To avoid getting fat.

Out from what seemed nowhere
A man came walking on by.
And this man did indeed give me
A purposeful wink of his eye.

I looked right up at him
From the bench where I sat.
He had a large letter *M*
Emblazoned upon his Hat.

His big hat was worn proudly.
It was very colorful and more.
Made of moisture wicking fibers.
Like nothing I'd seen before.

He then spoke out to me.
His voice was somewhat flat.
He just smiled and casually said,
"I'm the Motivator in the Hat."

II. "C'mon, C'mon!"

I thought he must be crazy
To introduce himself like that.
But he did seem so intriguing
This man with the weird funny hat.

He talked and seemed to know
I'd contemplated a run.

"Why do you sit there like that?
Just because there is no sun?"

I just looked up rather speechless
Not really certain what I should do.
I then decided I'd go for a run
And I began to lace my shoe.

Then my friend on the bench press
Looked at me and he did say,
"Go tell that guy in that strange hat
You won't play on a day like today.

"He should not tempt you
To get outside in the rain.
You're going to catch a cold
It all seems quite insane."

III. Closing the Deal

I admit it was a bit different.
I'd never seen this man before.
I just sat there staring at him
While I wavered on the floor.

He placed his hand upon my
    shoulder
And then spoke directly to me.
"I know sometimes it's hard to
    begin
And find that starting key."

"But you'll feel better for going
Even at times like these.
Approach all you do with zeal
Each day you must truly seize."

He said, "It's about experiencing
Everything you really can.
Don't let regret or hesitation
Ever be a part of your plan.

"I'll provide you words of advice
Experience I've gained day to day.
I'll fill you up with knowledge
For you to learn and file away."

I was more than a bit bewildered.
I wondered if I should call security.
But I opted to go running with
    him.
This baffling man and curious me.

I figured I'd nothing to lose
Running with him on that day.
If he got a little too kooky
I could always just sprint away.

I guess he was a motivating
    speaker
Perhaps working best upon his
    feet.
Messages conveyed while running
Rather than lecturing from a seat.

But his clothes were water
    repellant
Mine would only leave me
    sodden.
Even his shoes had some Gore-Tex
I felt a little downtrodden.

Reaching deep into a fancy bag
He advised I'd nothing to fear.
He pulled things out like magic
And gave me some waterproof
    gear.

He said, "It's losers who make
    excuses
While it's goals that winners make.
You must strive to accomplish
Each day for your own sake."

It was though he was
A coach sent to invigorate me.
He continued on with his pep talk
My own personal Knute Rockne.

Somehow he must have known
I'd been a bit down in the dump.
He was now here to help
Remove me from my slump.

IV. The Mystical Mystery Miles

A. Passing the Baton of Passion

Out we went and splashed about
It seemed an amazing run that
    day.
It was exhilarating to feel
Once again like a child at play.

He said, "It's not just with running
To proceed with a child's zest.
Bring an excitement to all things
And it will help you feel the best."

We ran across trails and over grass
And romped merrily through the
    street.
It seemed as though I had
A magical bounce within my feet.

He said, "Try inspirational music
Or the lure of a postrun treat.
There are many ways to get out
    the door.
My bag of tricks is quite replete.

"One way is to pick a race,
Train with that purpose in mind.

Set goals and monitor them
    closely
Excitement is what you'll find.

"Or run just to smell the flowers,
Hear the birds, and feel the wind
    blow.
Feel the exhilaration of activity,
Not the sloth of a couch potato."

He offered more words of advice.
He was excited to give me his spiel.
It seemed he enjoyed helping
    others
Stop spinning that proverbial
    wheel.

His message was if you kept
    spinning
You'd remain where you did start.
He talked of continuing to grow
That challenging yourself is
    what's smart.

I wasn't much for deep thinking.
Scholarly lessons weren't my forte.
But I couldn't help listening to him
As we ran on and on that day.

I was mesmerized by this man
And digested his words and
    thought.
Even running fast with oxygen debt
I was comprehending what he
    taught.

He said, "To get the most delight
Before you're laid to rest.
Just find great joy in one thing
To help live life to the best.

"Try out many different things.
You must often show persistence.
But discovering a real passion
Will only serve to enrich your
    existence."

Suddenly it dawned on me.
He was both smart and cunning.
He had determined that my
    passion
Should be found within my
    running.

I figured it wasn't going to be
Needlepoint, ceramics, or cooking.
I had always enjoyed my running
But a passion—I hadn't been
    looking.

He knew what I needed to hear
With all the words that he said.
His messages were quite subtle
Not like a hammer upon my head.

I kept listening intently
Not much more for me to do.
I just cruised along in silence
With this unusual running guru.

B. Don't Miss the Road to Bliss

"On days you need motivation
I know a good idea to send.
Think of some of your better runs,
The feelings during and at the end.

"Remember the pleasure you felt
Right there and then at that time.
It'll help you stay motivated
And make it easier you will find."

He had tricks up his CoolMax
  sleeve.
His ideas seemed to be quite sane
On days when thoughts of
  laziness
Were dancing all around my brain.

C. Means to Success

He said, "Some talk of endorphins
The sensation of a 'runners high'.
But those feelings of euphoria
Occur because you chose to try.

"It really is all quite simple
Just put forth effort like you
  should.
It's like that little choo choo train
In the book *The Little Engine That
  Could*.

"Keep a positive attitude
Especially as on you ran.
Recite the train's words of wisdom
For it said '**I think I can!**' "

He was now quoting children's
  stories
Not going deep with his
  philosophy.
He knew not to get that erudite
In conveying his messages to me.

He then gave me a little wink
As if knowing what was in my
  head.
And how to get through to me
With all the words that he said.

Well, all the power to him
If he could get inside my mind.

I often wondered what was in there
I was curious as to what he'd find.

D. Getting the Most from the Host

He then talked of training
Many ways to skin the same cat.
Find out what works best for you
Advised my Motivator in the Hat.

He told me if your running leaves
  you
Feeling both tired and drained.
You can be rest assured
That you have indeed overtrained.

He said, "If you're overly fatigued
Cut back on your miles and you
  shall see.
You'll begin feeling better
And get back your lost energy."

I'd have to admit that often
I'd train till I felt half-dead.
Even with my times getting slower
I'd continue on like a knucklehead.

E. Just When You Least Expect It

He then talked about something
That many of us did lack.
Knowing when to listen to pain
And then ease a little back.

"Runners often believe
They're immune from an injury.
When it occurs they bemoan,
'How could this have happened to
  me?'

"There are preventive measures
To make your running more
    constant.
Stretching your tendons and
    muscles
Will help keep you both flexible
    and pliant."

He then stopped running for a
    moment
Kicked his leg way above his head.
Told me I'd be just as limber
If I'd heed the words he'd said.

Now I was pretty impressed
With this flexibility sign.
He could kick about as high
As the Rockettes chorus line.

F. A Pace with Haste

He then talked about a skill
I thought someone had chosen to
    rescind.
That distant memory I had
Of actually running like the wind.

He said "If you want more speed
With training you can't be lax.
You need to do things like
    intervals
And learn about your VO_2max.

"Do workouts such as fartlek
Mix it up from day to day.
That term is a Swedish word
Meaning to do some speed play.

"It need not be painful
Pushing yourself can be a joy.

Delight in the feeling of swiftness
It's like finding a brand new toy.

"You'll get yourself moving faster
And gain the feel of being fleet.
By doing 400-meter repeats
It'll put some speed back in your
    feet."

I was getting more excited
It was going to be speed training
    or bust.
I knew my quickness wasn't all
    gone
I'd dust if off and remove the rust.

V. Which Way Did He Go?

We finished our spirited run
And he barely did perspire.
He'd just been gliding along
Trying to light my internal fire.

I realized that I'd been running fast
Ten miles had zipped right on by.
If I had this magic guy at races
I would really be able to fly.

He certainly had a way about him
With his manner and approach.
He was kind and encouraging
Part teacher, friend, and coach.

He said, "It's not all about winning
Although that's fun—I wouldn't lie.
But there's a thrill in just partici-
    pating
Not idly watching life go by."

I wanted to continue listening
To my helpful Motivator in the Hat.

But as suddenly as he'd appeared
He was gone as quick as a cat.

I'd been taking off my shoes
Turned and placed them on a mat.
When I moved back around
No more Motivator in the Hat.

But he'd left many messages
For me to carry through the
    miles.
Always relish your ability to run
Let it bring you nothing but
    smiles.

He stressed it's much better to fail
Than to never have even tried.
I was certain I'd always recall
All the motivation he supplied.

It then occurred to me
How his endurance had been so
    great.
He never appeared to be winded
At all on our running date.

Could the Hat have been super-
    natural?
Was it all that simple and plain?
I guess I really knew otherwise.
Great stamina came from how
    he'd train.

VI. Implementation and Execution

Having left me so inspired
I chose a marathon that I would
    run.
I'd follow his wise words of advice
It would all be so very fun.

I attempted to alter my diet
And try to watch all that I ate.
I began taking more vitamins
As well as glucosamine sulfate.

I did the required long runs
At a nice and comfortable rate.
I trained so on my marathon day
I wouldn't meet a horrible fate.

I became a well-oiled machine
And when my race was in but a
    week.
I knew that come that marathon
    day
I'd done all to be at my peak.

When the race did indeed arrive
I was focused and well grounded.
I recalled the shrewd Motivator in
    the Hat
And smiled as the starting gun
    sounded.

I stayed true to my anticipated pace
Keeping my adrenaline well within
    check.
I certainly knew if I didn't
I'd soon be a slow moving wreck.

I drank fluid at each aid station
Doing everything just right.
I was going to stay well hydrated
Replacing lost electrolytes.

I felt pretty good
As if I were in cruise control.
But I remained quite aware
Miles could ultimately take their toll.

I recalled the Motivator in the Hat
Saying with a wink and a sly
    smile.
"The race doesn't truly begin
Until you see the sign for
    the 20th mile.

"For it's then that your glycogen
Begins to get depleted.
But if you've done the training
You won't feel at all defeated.

"Indeed this is the area of legend
It's difficult to really explain.
Where runners may crash and
    burn
If they did not properly train.

"The legs begin to feel heavy
Your stride then starts shrinking.
Some second-guess themselves
    for entering
As they mumble 'What was I
    thinking?'

"But the last six miles
Need not really give you fits.
There are actually some runners
Who do run negative splits.

"That's when the second half of
    the race
Is run faster than the first.
They can finish it fairly strong
Not feeling as though they're
    cursed."

As I approached twenty miles
I thought about everything he
    did say.

I was convinced I'd be okay
For I'd done it all the right way.

He'd taught me many tricks
Things to do to feel very well.
It was now at this juncture
That I swallowed some energy gel.

Now, I won't tell you it was easy
I won't say it was a piece of cake.
It required tremendous exertion
And all the effort I could make.

I remember what he'd told me,
"There are runners of all kind.
But everyone reaches a worthy
    goal
When they cross the finish line.

"It's then one realizes
The pleasure in pursuing a goal.
And the rapture of accomplishing it
Gets right down deep into your
    soul.

"If a marathon were simple
Then everyone would do it with
    ease.
Some run fast and some run slow
But you need to do as you please.

"Some take many, many hours
Others run for the fastest time.
But goals are all relative
There'll be yours and also be
    mine."

With only one mile to go
I grabbed my last drink from a
    cup.

I tried to mount a finishing kick
But I had lactic acid buildup.

I then heard spectators' applause
And knew the finish line was in
    sight.
Since I was still moving forward
I guess I was doing all right.

I went across the finish line
I'd passed this endurance test.
I looked up at the clock and saw
I'd also beaten my personal best!

I hoped someday I'd see my
    friend
To thank him for what he'd done.
He rekindled with me a passion
He'd made my life more fun.

Perhaps I'd become just like him.
Maybe that is where it's at.
Spreading his word throughout
    the land.
A disciple of Motivator in the Hat.

I can't call myself the same thing
So maybe the *Encourager in a
    Cap*.
Perhaps give my thoughts and
    suggestions
In a catchy soulful rap.

Maybe I'd get some people
To enjoy their own victory dance.
But his point was about more
    than winning
It was being willing to take the
    chance.

VII. The Last Lesson

But he also gave one final message
That I know I'll never forget.
It was different from all the others
I haven't even touched upon it yet.

Maybe you believe he isn't real
Perhaps think he's but a rumor.
But I say the final lesson he gave me
Was never lose your sense of
    humor.

With all his earnest words of advice
That he wanted me to see.
He'd also stressed to not forget
That laughter's very much a key.

I figured with that silly hat
He also had a comedic side.
It all meant having balance
Just relax and enjoy the ride.

So be dedicated but not obsessed
With running or whatever's your
    thing.
He said that your success in life
Is in the smiles to others you bring.

About the Author

Bob Schwartz is a freelance writer. In addition to his humorous slice of life column, which has appeared hundreds of times in magazines and newspapers throughout the country, he is well known to the running community. His funny essays on running have been published in national and regional magazines, including *Runner's World, FootNotes, Fitness Runner, Michigan Runner, New York Runner, Running Fitness (United Kingdom), Washington Running Report, Tail Winds, Run Ohio, Midwest Running, Race Center NW, Arkansas Runner, Oklahoma Runner, Inside Texas Running, Running Journal, Missouri Runner, Florida Running & Triathlon, Rocky Mountain Sports, Windy City Sports, Twin Cities Sports, Metro Sports Magazine, Texas Health & Fitness, Pennsylvania Health & Fitness.* Schwartz also presents comical speeches at race expos.

An avid runner for more than twenty-five years, Schwartz has run over twenty marathons and race distances from the 200 Meter Kids Snowman Shuffle to ultramarathons. In the universal language of runners, he has PR's of 2:42 for the marathon, 34:18 for 10K, 1:16 for the half marathon and 56 seconds for the third grade potato sack race.

Schwartz lives in Huntington Woods, Michigan with his wife Robin and three children. He can be reached at rschwartz@s4online.com.

About the Illustrator

B. K. Taylor is a well-known illustrator and writer who has contributed to such varied media as National Lampoon, Walt Disney Animations, Jim Henson Productions, MAD, Scholastic, Nickelodeon, and ABC's Home Improvement (staff writer). He currently serves as creative director of the entertainment division of SV-3 Media.

Taylor's work has been recognized with the Inkpot Award, the Gold Brick, seven Caddies, the Funny Bone Award and the Ace Award.

Taylor lives in Franklin, Michigan with his wife, Kathleen, two daughters, and Rudy the Wonder Dog, who sleeps under his drawing board. B. K.'s leisure activities include traveling, hiking, art collecting and part-time crime fighting.